The Pickle Clowns

THE PICKLE CLOWNS

New American Circus Comedy

Edited and with Interviews by

Joel Schechter

SOUTHERN ILLINOIS UNIVERSITY PRESS
Carbondale and Edwardsville

Printed in the United States of America

04 03 02 01   4 3 2 1

Book design: Gary Gore

Library of Congress Cataloging-in-Publication Data
The pickle clowns : new American circus comedy / edited and with interviews by Joel
Schechter.
    p. cm.
Includes bibliographical references and index.
1. Pickle Family Circus. 2. Clowns—Interviews. I. Schechter, Joel, date.
GV1811.A1 P53 2001
791.3'3—dc21

                                                                    00-050472

ISBN 0-8093-2357-5 (pbk. : alk. paper)

The paper used in this publication meets the minimum requirements of American
National Standard for Information Sciences—Permanence of Paper for Printed Library
Materials, ANSI Z39.48-1992. ⊗

For the Pickles

Contents

Illustrations

Preface

In the circus ring, clowns display extraordinary invention and freedom. At their finest, they disrupt the ringmaster's expectations and ours with comic anarchy, exquisite physical movement, satiric dialogue, songs, eccentric dance, and nonsense. In circus books, including their own books, clowns tend to be more restrained. Memoirs by the great English clown Joseph Grimaldi and Albert Fratellini's recollections of clowning in Paris reveal almost nothing about their most outrageous and popular acts. Rather than write it all down, circus comedians are more likely to describe the details of their art in conversation with family members and close friends and privately teach their acts to a few performers.

Fortunately for the rest of us, clown conversations have been recorded and printed, some as early as 1850, when journalist Henry Mayhew transcribed interviews with a street clown, a penny-gaff clown, a canvas clown, and a penny-circus jester. The oral tradition through which clowns pass their art to one another became more widely accessible with the publication of Mayhew's oral histories in *London Labour and the London Poor*. His superb interviews with comic "street exhibitors" were part of a larger survey that gave new public voice and dignity, as well as written history, to artists whose work might otherwise have disappeared as soon as their performances ended.

I am indebted to Mayhew's exemplary interviews and to the achievements of the French circus historian Tristan Rémy, who transcribed and published scenarios for many of Europe's finest clown acts in his book *Entrées clownesques*. This collection of scenarios and Rémy's biographical essays in *Les Clowns* constitute landmarks in the field of clown history; they have yet to be matched by English language writers, although books by Ernest Albrecht, Ron Jenkins, Laurence Senelick, John Towsen, David Wiles, and Don Wilmeth have taken commendable steps in that direction.

I would not dare compare my collection of Pickle clown interviews to the masterful achievements of Mayhew and Rémy, except to say that the method—of oral history and circus act transcription—was inspired by them. In its own modest way, this volume attempts to continue the preservation of clown history that Mayhew and Rémy pioneered.

My book could not have been completed without the generous cooperation of all the artists interviewed. I am grateful for their superb comic creations and their willingness to discuss their art with me. In some cases, they recalled events that had occurred twenty-five years before we spoke, and I had the pleasure of recovering—or seeing them recover—lost and forgotten circus acts. It was almost like being at the circus again.

A note on terminology is necessary. While the Pickle clowns share some attributes of the elegant, smart whiteface and the stupid, shabbily dressed *auguste* clowns well known in European circus tradition, the Pickles rarely used such terms to describe themselves in our conversations. I follow their example in my introductory essay and avoid debating who was the *auguste* and who the whiteface when I consider the diverse traditions and originality of their circus comedy.

Support and encouragement for my research were provided by Jim Mayer at Ideas in Motion; Margaret Norton and the librarians at San Francisco's Performing Arts Library and Museum (PALM); the New Pickle Circus office, particularly Nancy Matheson, Pat Osbon, and Tandy Beal; San Francisco School of Circus Arts cofounders Wendy Parkman and Judy Finelli; photographer Terry Lorant; and San Francisco State University, which granted me sabbatical time to engage in what Geoff Hoyle would call "the archeology of pratfalls." I am grateful to friends and colleagues who offered me advice, including clown historians Ron Jenkins and Laurence Senelick, circus journal editor Ernest Albrecht, and my circus-going partner, Diana Scott. I want to acknowledge the work of critics who saw the Pickle clowns before I did (I missed a few openings) and whose lively accounts I read. They include Ernest Albrecht, Michael Billington, Jon Carroll, Alfred Frankenstein, Robert Hurwitt, Nancy Scott, Irving Wardle, Bernard Weiner, and Steven Winn. Thanks also to Southern Illinois University Press and editors James Simmons, Carol Burns, and Julie Bush, who have enabled the Pickle clowns to be heard and seen once again.

The Pickle Clowns

Four Pickle clowns *(from left):* Lorenzo Pickle (Larry Pisoni), Ms. Wombat (Andrea Snow), Willy the Clown (Bill Irwin), and Mr. Sniff (Geoff Hoyle). Photo by Terry Lorant.

Introducing
the Pickle Clowns

THE NAMES of great circus clowns are hardly known in our country. Fratellini, Grock, and Durov are not names you hear in everyday dinner conversation, unless you are a clown. In other countries, in other times, their names were celebrated, their acts revered.

Today, circus clowns are an endangered species; their live physical comedy receives far less public support than acts that are no longer alive but are prerecorded on film and television. While there have been movements to save the whale and the owl from threats of extinction, the circus clown (a kind of loon) and its wild life in the ring have few preservationists speaking on their behalf.

The lives and acts of European clowns were preserved half a century ago by the French circus historian Tristan Rémy in his books *Les Clowns* and *Entrées clownesques.* American clowns deserve to have their history and scenarios documented in detail, too, since their artistry rivals that of the Europeans. Beginning with the New York–born clown Dan Rice and his "one-horse show" in the nineteenth century, and continuing through the twentieth-century antics of Lou Jacobs, Otto Griebling, and Emmett Kelly in the Ringling Bros. and Barnum & Bailey arena to the new wave of clowns in the Pickle Family Circus, the Big Apple Circus, Circus Flora, and Cirque du Soleil, many superbly gifted comedians have passed through North American circus tents.

More than one volume would be needed to record the full history of our country's clowns (and I am not even thinking of politicians who might fit into this category). The Pickle clowns featured here are not the only ones deserving attention, but their achievements as a group offer an exemplary model of new American circus comedy that is all too quickly disappearing in the age of electronic entertainment. In our era of globalization, when the Ringling Bros. and Barnum & Bailey circus continues to call itself "the greatest show on earth" and a television program bills itself as "The Circus of the Stars," a small circus with a few clowns and no stars except those in the sky above its open-air arena offered audiences great beauty, adventure, and comedy, live and in person.

The Pickle clowns introduced here had the privilege of performing in the last twenty-five years of the twentieth century, at a time when live comedy and small circuses faced tremendous competition from television and film. An announcement of a comic performance by, say, Robin Williams "live and in person" could still attract an enormous audience. But to attract that audience, the comedian first had to become well known through film or television broadcasts. As the critic Walter Benjamin once observed, "It is inherent in the technique of the film . . . that everybody who witnesses its accomplishments is somewhat of an expert."[1] When clowns perform live in a one-ring circus and are seen by a small audience surrounding their space rather than on camera, most of the public has no "expert" knowledge of them. Their pratfalls, dances, and comic dialogue can still be appreciated by spectators who see the clowns in person for the first time; one doesn't have to be an expert to laugh at the spaghetti routine performed by Bill Irwin and Geoff Hoyle. (The number of people who saw this spaghetti plate juggling act increased considerably when Irwin performed a version of it on Broadway in his 1993 stage show, *Fool Moon.*) While such acts deserve a larger audience, the Pickle clowns originally thrived in a one-ring circus where the limited seating capacity was an asset, as it contributed to the intimacy and immediacy of their comic art. Audience members were almost in the show themselves. They sat close to the performers—there was no other location available—and the clowns would not let the audience forget this as they personally greeted spectators and threatened to toss a cream pie in the public's direction.

When the Pickle Family Circus officially opened in May 1975 at the O'Connell High School gym in San Francisco, its presentation was so new it looked old. Covering the premiere for the *San Francisco Examiner,* journalist Carol Pogash mistakenly reported, "They are what circuses probably were before they reached the big time."[2] Pogash was correct insofar as earlier American circuses had been small in size, before three- and five-ring spectacles became more common; but few if any early American circuses were clown-centered cooperatives performing without a tent and without animals. The Pickle Family Circus's innovative, animal-free acts in a small space were at the forefront of a whole movement of "New Circus." Other new one-ring circuses in North America followed, including the Big Apple, Circus Flora, and Cirque du Soleil.

But none of the others began with a group of clowns as gifted as Larry Pisoni, Bill Irwin, and Geoff Hoyle—the trio known in the ring as Lorenzo Pickle, Willy the Clown, and Mr. Sniff. In the first years of their circus, these three created a comic style that might be called "Fratellini American." The Pickle clowns revitalized the art of the *entrée* (an extended clown act, complete with dialogue), which clowns like the trio of Albert, Paul, and François Fratellini popularized at Cirque Medrano in Paris half a century earlier.[3] In the 1970s and later, when the clowns at Ringling Bros. often went into their three rings simply to cover scene changes, the Pickle clowns were the main act in one open-air ring. Critics who saw the first Pickle clowns compared them to Keaton, Chaplin, and the Marx Brothers but rarely to other circus clowns, because most comparable clowns were in Europe and unknown to Americans. Cirque du Soleil has become more popular and far wealthier than the Pickle circus in recent years; but the Pickle clowns and their *entrées* continue to have few equals in North America.

Since 1975, there have been many changes in the Pickle Family Circus and its clown repertoire. The artists to whom I refer as the Pickle clowns are not all still in the circus. Even the circus name has changed; it became the New Pickle Circus in 1993, when it reorganized under bankruptcy proceedings, and it has not offered a full season of performances recently, only special events. Late in 2000, the New Pickle Circus reunited with its former affiliate, the San Francisco School of Circus Arts, and a new artistic director, Lu Yi, was appointed.[4] Most of the clowns discussed here have left the Pickles to perform comedy in theatres, dance concerts, one-person shows, television, and film. Still, that a small circus could produce so many popular clowns in its first twenty-five years makes its history and that of its clowns extraordinary.

When clowns leave the circus, they take their acts with them, or create new acts. As a result, many of the clown numbers created for San Francisco's Pickle Family Circus survive only as history, preserved in rare videotapes, scattered newspaper reviews, and photographs. I confess there are some Pickle clown acts I never saw. That was one reason I set out to bring their trios and duos together again in this volume. To recover and preserve their lost acts, I constructed texts with their dialogue and stage directions, and I interviewed most of the clowns. Lorenzo Pickle, Willy the Clown, Ramona the Tap-Dancing Gorilla, Mr. Sniff, Ms. Wombat, Queenie Moon, Ralph, Pino, and Razz are all present—or at least their words are—in the pages that follow.

Voices are a start, but these clowns were and are superb physical comedians. Their body language often has said more than their words; their falls, trips, flips, and double takes spoke volumes. Unfortunately, they could not be here in person today.

Circus clowns have never been famous for their conversation, at least not until now. In some circuses, such as Ringling Bros. and Barnum & Bailey, clowns are hardly ever heard. They enter a three-ringed arena and perform brief, wordless interludes, throw buckets of confetti, and chase one another until the tiger cage or the trapeze has been set up for the next act. The Pickle clowns are different. They speak audibly from the center ring—their only ring—and they address the audience as well as one another. They are not there to cover scene changes but to run the circus, more or less, as they replace the traditional ringmaster and introduce and perform the featured acts.

The Pickle clowns were not the first American comics to speak in the ring. In the nineteenth century, Dan Rice was famous for his spoken parodies of Shakespearean dialogue, for example.[5] But as circus size increased from one ring to three and five rings, the large crowds and cavernous spaces made it difficult to be heard. (Body microphones are now used by some circuses; but in the past, when clowns performed without advanced electronic equipment, much of the audience was not close to ringside.)

The first words of the Pickle Family Circus clowns were heard in 1975 when Larry Pisoni and Bill Irwin served spectators the comic number called *Spaghetti,* complete with droll dialogue about rigatoni, macaroni, ravioli, and other pasta. The text of the act, revised when Geoff Hoyle joined in a year later, constitutes what European circus clowns call an *entrée,* not because it concerns food but because it is a main entry in the program, a one-act play in the ring. These playlets with distinct characters usually last ten to twenty minutes, although the famous Fratellini were known to present forty-five-minute *entrées,* frequently lengthened by audience laughter.

The best of the Pickle Family Circus *entrées* renew the popular European form of comedy that Grock, Dario and Bario, Rhum and Pipo, Tonio and Lulu, and the Fratellini trio created in the first half of the twentieth century. (As their names suggest, a number of the European clowns had Italian family origins, like Lorenzo Pickle.) Some of the French, Swiss, and Italian *entrées* have been translated into English in a volume titled *Clown Scenes,* from Tristan Rémy's anthology, *Entrées clownesques.* Few American equivalents can be found in print. Reluctance by clowns to publish such comic material is understandable, since some of the humor based on physical comedy is lost in print and lost if lesser comedians read and copy the act. In the case of American clowns, there is also a scarcity of *entrées* because larger circuses discouraged extended clown acts with dialogue and theatrical characters in them.

Over the past quarter century, since Lorenzo Pickle and Willy the Clown first spoke about pasta, other clown *entrées* have been created by them and by Mr. Sniff (Geoff Hoyle), Queenie Moon and Ralph (Joan Mankin and Donald Forrest), Ms. Wombat (Andrea Snow), and Pino and Razz (Diane Wasnak and Jeff Raz). The characters these clowns portray are not always masters of language; they trip over words with nonsense, puns, mispronunciations, and neologisms, verbal counterparts of physical pratfalls and juggling. And sometimes they say nothing at all but simply step inside storage trunks or play musical instruments after much difficulty in setting up their concert chairs.

THE UTOPIA OF CLOWNS

Although the Pickle clowns misuse and misunderstand language in their comic acts, they proved to be quite articulate when I interviewed them. Their recollections vividly describe a world of surreal imagination and physical comedy with all the enthusiasm of those who lived in a clown utopia.

Their circus was a clown utopia, a place loved by and for its clowns, a comic realm found nowhere else, at least in one respect. The Pickles endured hardships on the road and off, but their interviews construct an open-air circus in which clowns thrived and ran the show because they could talk outside the ring with one another and with circus directors to develop acts that allowed their senses of humor, their bodies, and their voices full play. (It also helped that one of the cofounders of the circus, Larry Pisoni, was a lead clown *and* artistic director for twelve years.) Circus cofounder and juggler Peggy Snider told me that from the beginning, the circus performances were built around the clown acts.[6] The clown *entrées* were given about half the show's time as recently as 1998 in the holiday show, *Step Right Up!* As the Pickle clown trios and duos stayed together over several seasons, they had far more time for ensemble development of their comedy than do actors in regional theatres, who rehearse for four to six weeks and separate after a month of performance.

What I call utopia here may have been expected, or even ordinary, to some European clowns in the 1920s. However, I doubt that there are many American clowns, besides the Pickles, who would recall their circus days as favorably as Joan Mankin did when she told me, "The important thing about working as a clown in the Pickles was that you really had a voice in the shaping of the circus. The circus developed around the clowns."[7] That voice, or those voices, can be heard in the conversations that follow.

Not all the clown acts depended on spoken dialogue. It would be misleading to suggest that verbal facility was the most popular part of the clowning. The Pickle clowns were adept as mimes, acrobats, jugglers, slack-rope walkers, and dancers, which gave them tremendous physical gifts for their *entrées*. They frequently worked with the choreographers Kimi Okada and Tandy Beal, also interviewed in this volume; and some of their clown acts would qualify as eccentric dances. (Beal simultaneously served as artistic director of the New Pickle Circus and of her own dance company.) The live music of the circus band tended to accentuate the choreographed aspects of the clowning. Circus music director and composer Jeffrey Gaeto once said the Pickle band's music turned the circus "into one long dance."[8]

PICKLES PRESERVED

The Pickle clowns have been highly praised in the past. Critics who saw Hoyle, Irwin, and Pisoni perform *The Three Musicians* and other *entrées* together would refer to them as three of the greatest American clowns of the century. Jon Carroll, the *San Francisco Chronicle* columnist (and a speech writer for clown Queenie Moon), wrote in his 1985 program notes for the *Pickle Clown Reunion* that the period when the trio of Pisoni, Hoyle, and Irwin performed "was arguably . . . the most amazing moment in the history of 20th Century American circus, three great clowns making each other greater."[9] Perhaps he exaggerated; earlier in the century, the American clowns Lou Jacobs, Otto Griebling, and Emmett Kelly were also quite remarkable (though not in the same act), and many American circus artists who were not clowns also deserve high praise. A more modest but still laudatory appraisal comes from Ernest Albrecht in his 1995 book, *The New American Circus:* "Over the years the Pickle Family Circus numbered among its members some of America's most outstanding clowning talents. . . . A twenty-minute clown act would have been unthinkable in an American circus before this trio [Pisoni, Irwin, and Hoyle] of extraordinary clowns came together in one company."[10]

Critics who saw Mankin and Forrest or Raz and Wasnak perform together later praised them for sustaining the high comic standards (or high standards of comedy?) set by earlier Pickle clowns. "Their clown routines are skillfully executed classics," critic Robert Hurwitt wrote about Queenie

Moon and Ralph in May 1988. In December of 1992, he found Pino and Razz to be "a perfect pair," clowns "whose command of the craft recalls the golden Pickle era of Bill Irwin and Geoff Hoyle."[11]

Inevitably, unavoidably, past praise for the Pickle clowns has included puns on the name of their circus. Since they are unavoidable, they might as well be introduced now; they are almost as popular as the clowns: "Sweet Pickles" (Robert Hurwitt); "La Dolce Pickle" (Tandy Beal); "There's a new brand of Pickle, but don't be jarred" (Nancy Scott); "You don't have to be dill or kosher to be a pickle" (Harry McFarland); "I wish I were a Pickle" (Doris Lessing); "A Pickle for Your Thoughts" (Robert Hurwitt); "A Dill of a Show" (*San Jose Mercury News*).[12] Yes, these clowns and their colleagues are Pickles to relish.

Like other performing arts, clowning is ephemeral; nothing can fully recapture the original conditions of its presentation. Although I regard Terry Lorant's photographs as the finest visual records of the acts available—documents full of the humor and startling beauty of the original acts—one can only imagine what it was like to sit near the Pickle clowns and watch them disappear in storage trunks, juggle plates of spaghetti, play tubas and saxophones in duets, or dance with a gorilla chorus line outdoors, accompanied by live band music, children of all ages, widespread laughter, and applause.

All of the artists interviewed here have gone on to perform in other arenas—dance, theatre, and performance art—to acclaim across the country; and in that work, as they admit in interviews, their Pickle clown experience continues to affect their work. Bill Irwin notes about the clowning he has done with other Pickles, "It is not only still alive, but for something so ephemeral, you would think it would bear very little resemblance to what somebody was doing 30, 40, 150 years ago, but books suggest that there's a great resemblance." The Pickle clowns are now without question part of a larger comic tradition, extending (in books and play texts, where it survives) from Aristophanes to the Zanni of Italian *commedia,* Shakespeare's fools, Dario Fo and Franca Rame's satiric subversives, Beckett's clown tramps, and the clown jugglers of "New Vaudeville." It is a tradition that the Pickles now enlarge through their circus-influenced performances of plays by Shakespeare, Jonson, Molière, Feydeau, O'Casey, Beckett, Brecht, Fo, and Rame, as well as postmodern dance and their own theatrical solos.

The clowns may not be quite as funny in their interviews as they are in the ring; but they are erudite (if that is any compensation for diminished humor) and versed in the history of comic performance. For better or worse (better, I think), this knowledge makes them different from earlier clowns. How many earlier circus clowns were able to learn from Italian *commedia*, Elizabethan fools, Beckett, and Brecht *and* Jackie Gleason, Lucille Ball, Peking opera, and the San Francisco Mime Troupe? (Larry Pisoni was seen reading a book on the semiotics of circus in the late 1970s. That could have been a clown act, except that the reading took place in private, outside the ring.)

These artists have seen more and drawn from a wider body of cultural experience than their predecessors. (Of course, they had more to choose from.) Many of them came to the circus from theatre or dance ensembles and fused other art forms with their clowning. If it is a "postmodern" tendency for performers to quote diverse traditions and techniques within their work, to draw on Kabuki and Buster Keaton at the same time, then perhaps these clowns are postmodern. I think they might be inclined to parody such terms. (I can hear Queenie Moon's squeaky voice now: "Did he say postmortem?") If name-calling is in order, they have far more amusing names for themselves.

Asked how the Pickle Family Circus acquired its name, Larry Pisoni recalls that his group of jugglers, composed of Peggy Snider, Cecil MacKinnon, and himself, performed without a name until a New York television producer asked who they were. Pisoni looked at his female partners and replied: "We're definitely not Pickle Brothers." This denial was followed by a decision that they were the Pickle Family Jugglers and later led them to the name Pickle Family Circus.

The addition of the word "Family" turned the Pickles into a parody of the great Italian and Russian circus dynasties (Fratellini, Durov) in which children and grandchildren continued the profession of their ancestors. Peggy Snider called herself Peggy Pickle, Cecil MacKinnon called herself

Sally Pickle, and Larry Pisoni became Lorenzo Pickle. One early favorable circus review written by Alfred Frankenstein for the *San Francisco Chronicle* in July 1976 refers to Lorenzo, Sally, and Peggy Pickle as if they were born with those names.[13] (Over the past two decades, Larry Pisoni and Peggy Snider's children have become highly accomplished adult circus artists, but they do not use "Pickle" as their family name.)

In a delightful essay on the Pickles, my colleague and fellow clown historian Ron Jenkins once wrote that the "circus skills displayed by the [Pickle] troupe are admirable, but it is the simple, decent family values inherent in their execution that make the show unique," as everyone in the audience begins to wish "they had a father who could do pratfalls, a mother who could juggle, a sister who could do back flips in the air."[14] While I agree with Jenkins that the Pickles became a "family circus" of that sort over the years, the initial choice of the words "Pickle Family" for their name was inspired more by a joke about Pickle Brothers than by decent circus family values.

Knowing the story behind the name also rules out speculation that it began with reference to the circus size (*piccolo* or "small" in Italian) or the favorite food of the clowns. Del Monte's Genuine Dills were once advertised in the program as the "Official Pickle of the Pickle Family Circus."[15] In that sense, some of the circus pickles were preserved, in jars, for future appreciation without use of photography or recorded interviews.

DANCING GORILLAS ENTER

When the circus first opened in May 1975, it featured two clown acts as well as the Pickle Family Jugglers, unicyclists, and acrobats. One clown act mentioned earlier introduced Willy the Clown as a waiter and Lorenzo Pickle as a restaurant chef. (The text of this *entrée, Spaghetti,* is reprinted later.)

The other clown act had Bill Irwin portray an animal trainer, Hauptman von Clown, whose gorilla took away his cane and forced him to tap-dance. Ramona La Mona the Tap-Dancing Gorilla, played by Kimi Okada, was the first of many animals impersonated by humans in the otherwise animal-free circus.

The gorilla and trainer tap dance also was the first step (or steps) the circus took in the field of comic dance. Later, other clowns danced, and not only in the gorilla chorus line choreographed by Okada. (Her popular ensemble of nine gorillas in ruffled, polka-dot collars premiered at the circus in 1983.) Forms of dance theatre and eccentric dance were quite prominent when Tandy Beal directed her first full-length circus show, *Tossing and Turning*, in 1992.

Before they saw the Pickles (and animal-free Cirque du Soleil, which in 1984 followed the Pickles' lead), many Americans regarded a circus as a series of spectacular, death-defying feats performed by animals and humans inside a ring (or three rings). Animals were present at the creation of the first circus ring in 1768, when British sergeant-major Philip Astley turned a riding arena into a public performance space for equestrian acts. He designed a ring (about forty-two feet in diameter) regarded as optimal for horse maneuvers in front of a seated audience. Animals and their riders were the main attraction. Astley was his circus's first clown, in a comic act performed on horseback. Since then, clowns and trained animals have frequently appeared in the circus, in the same act or separately.

While other circuses face charges that they mistreat their bears or elephants, the Pickles celebrate only human feats, even if some of the humans are dressed like gorillas (and once like a lummox). The decision not to include live animal acts helped distinguish the Pickles from other larger circuses.

As noted earlier, the Pickles were at the forefront of the movement now known as "New Circus" or "New Wave Circus," in which artists ceased to use animal acts, multiple rings, and the traditional variety act structure. They departed from earlier preferences for three-ring spectacle, which by 1932 led circus historian Earl Chapin May to write, "Modern Americans do not want a one-ring show."[16] Ringling Bros. and Barnum & Bailey has continued to advertise great, greater, and greatest shows within three rings, although in 1999 even they admitted that one-ring circuses are attracting a new generation of circus-goers and added to their touring companies a one-ring tent show named Barnum's Kaleidoscape, with the gifted Italian clown David

Larible in a leading role. At the end of the twentieth century, the environmental movement's slogan "Small is beautiful" also had meaning for artists and audiences of the circus world. Cirque du Soleil and the Big Apple Circus chose to use one ring after the Pickles demonstrated the advantages of the small, intimate arena. It would be misleading to suggest that the Pickle Family Circus alone inspired new interest in the single-ring circus space or other advances. Other circuses in the United States and Europe had used only one ring before the Pickles. However, few of them had an animal-free and tent-free show *and* featured clown duos and trios.

The Pickle Family Circus also deserves plaudits for placing women in lead clown roles, a practice not common in circuses even today. Judy Finelli, the Pickle circus director who brought Joan Mankin and Diane Wasnak together as partners in 1989, has said that the two were the only female clown duo featured in a circus when they performed.[17] Larry Pisoni's comment that "We're definitely not Pickle Brothers" proved to be prophetic in this regard. Besides Mankin and Wasnak, Kimi Okada, Cecil MacKinnon, Andrea Snow, Peggy Snider, Wendy Parkman, Judy Finelli, Sara Felder, Sharon Ostreicher, and Stephanie Thompson have performed in Pickle clown acts, although some of them (MacKinnon, Snider, Finelli, Felder) were better known as comic jugglers and one (Parkman) as an aerialist.

The Pickle Family Circus was also different from the beginning because it performed outdoors in the open air, in daylight, with canvas sidewalls and a ground cover but no roof, for many seasons. (Big Apple, Cirque du Soleil, and other "New Circuses" did not follow suit; they still employ tents. The New Pickle Circus also now performs under cover, usually in roofed theatres.) Much like the San Francisco Mime Troupe, in which the Pickle cofounders had worked, the original Pickle Family Circus featured California sunlight as one of its special effects. The blues, reds, and yellows of costumes and canvas drops were heightened by beautifully lit greenery of the surrounding parks in which the circus performed. French circus historian Pascal Jacob has noted that the "New Circus" of the 1970s initially developed in the street and open spaces, when artists left more formal, traditional performance settings for locations where a large sector of the public might converge.[18]

The Pickle Family Jugglers (Pisoni, Snider, MacKinnon) learned how to attract and hold an audience outdoors several years before they started the circus. Peggy Snider noted that this juggling experience influenced the design of the first Pickle Family Circus sidewalls and bleacher seating;[19] the semicircular structure and daylight allowed audience members to laugh with and see one another while watching the acts, as they had while watching the comic jugglers perform in parks. (Audiences indoors in a tent or arena where special lights focus on the acts and keep spectators in the dark would not have the same experience.)

The circus audience was meant to be seen, not only to see. In a sense, spectators became performers, too, as they watched one another. In May of 1975, when the first show was over, the musicians played on, and audience members were free to step into the ring and dance. Audience acts influenced the clown acts, too, as Geoff Hoyle noted: "Early on we decided that in the open air, with an audience that was constantly in movement and had a multigenerational spread, many verbal gags were not going to work. We had a hard time being heard outdoors in the ring, although we found ways to be heard there, by making the speeches short and making them repeat key ideas." (Some politicians would benefit from following the same advice.)

In the San Francisco Bay Area, the history behind outdoor performances was not simply a search for new audiences or new performance space, however; it also had a political component, as antiwar marches in the 1960s and radical theatre performances in the parks had been bringing many people with political concerns together. It could be argued that at times, the political protests were like circuses, or at least entertaining spectacles. Bay Area activists Jerry Rubin and Wavy Gravy developed comic protest scenarios with pigs, costumes, and face paint. But the Pickle clowns were not simply following in the footsteps of Rubin or Gravy; for one thing, Hoyle, Irwin, and Pisoni wore bigger shoes.

GROUCHO MARXISTS

The Pickle preference for open-air performance recalls a San Francisco Mime Troupe poster declaring that the group favored "engagement, commitment, and fresh air." The Pickles too favored fresh air, without question. "Engagement" and "commitment" by the circus, particularly its clowns, require further discussion.

When Larry Pisoni was an actor in the San Francisco Mime Troupe from 1971 to 1973, he began to teach other troupers circus skills. His enthusiasm for juggling spread and enabled the actors to perform a new play, *Frozen Wages,* in which club-passing became a metaphor for factory production speedup. (Pisoni in his interview credits Mime Troupe director Dan Chumley and playwright Joan Holden for "largely" creating the 1972 play's scenario.)

Pisoni had learned juggling earlier in New York, from his mentor, Hovey Burgess, and his Electric Circus partner, Judy Finelli. (She joined the Pickles as a juggler in 1982, later to direct the circus school and then the circus itself.) Both Burgess and Finelli deserve some credit for the juggling renaissance that developed in San Francisco. But the cast list for the Mime Troupe production of *Frozen Wages* reads almost like a "Who's Who in Bay Area Juggling, 1972." Among the play's actors, besides Pisoni, were Merle Goldstone (soon to juggle with the Bay City Reds) and Michael Christensen (later to be lead clown at Big Apple and juggling partner of Big Apple founder Paul Binder) as well as future Pickles Michael Nolan, Joan Mankin, Peggy Snider, and Andrea Snow.

Besides learning to juggle in the Mime Troupe, these future circus artists acquired experience in comic acting. The political comedies of the Mime Troupe drew on the theatre of Brecht and *commedia dell'arte,* and its topical satires were energized by the civil rights and antiwar movements of the 1960s. (The Mime Troupe had a "Gorilla Marching Band" that performed in antiwar parades; however, unlike the Pickles in gorilla suits, the Mime Troupe gorillas were ragtag musicians who look, in some early photographs, like Vietnamese army guerrillas.)

Although many of the Pickles were once members of the Mime Troupe or, in Geoff Hoyle's case, had contemplated joining the troupe, their circus acts were rarely overtly political or topical, as Mime Troupe plays had been and still are. Bill Irwin, who was not in the Mime Troupe, recalls that while he was in the Pickle Family Circus, "one of the important struggles for me was to come to terms with . . . the political ethos of the time, and especially the subculture, the San Francisco Mime Troupe. . . . I was looking for a way to reflect a political outlook but at the same time trying to make fun of the self-serious 'lefter than thou' attitude of our subculture." When I mentioned that one of his clown act jokes about a "wage slave" slyly makes fun of political rhetoric, Irwin responded, "It's an old Marxist joke—Groucho's, I think."

Joan Mankin tells a funny story about working in a shipyard after leaving the Mime Troupe, because "we had been doing all these shows about the proletariat, and I had no idea what the proletariat was." The shipyard experience led her and former Mime Troupe actor Donald Forrest to create the Pickle clown act in which she comes home from a hard day of work. Wearing overalls, work boots, and a hard hat, she insists that her husband cook dinner. The resulting comedy in *Ralph and Queenie's Kitchen* is one example of circus clowning that reflected timely concerns about the changing roles of women in the workplace and at home.

In discussion of these issues, Mankin quite accurately notes that while most of the Pickle circus acts "weren't political comedy . . . their roots were very much based in the politics of that time. The circus had community group sponsors, and many of the groups were independent, progressive schools set up and run by people who were influenced by the Mime Troupe. They definitely used the same community. Of course, the circus wasn't as political as the Mime Troupe, because, thankfully, Larry [Pisoni] didn't want to have the circus be too dogmatic or theoretical."

Pisoni said as much himself when he told me that while he was quite excited and inspired by the Mime Troupe's work on political issues, he could remember "sitting at Joan Holden and Dan Chumley's kitchen table in the early '70s and saying, 'All I really want to do is make people laugh.'" So he became a clown. (He was a comic juggler before he became a clown or a Mime Troupe actor, it should be noted; the art of juggling is also quite capable of making people laugh.)

Another difference between Mime Troupe satire and Pickle circus clowning is suggested by Donald Forrest: "In the Mime Troupe, we had all these ideas that it's important, politically correct, for characters to realize where they're at and to metamorphose. The character should change. But in my experience in clowning, I realized that once you put on a mask, or clown makeup, that's who you are; it doesn't change. Clowns can influence the world around them to evolve or metamorphose, but the clowns remain constant."

Forrest's assessment of circus clowns as unchanging characters could be debated, but it applies to the Pickle clowns insofar as their characters were set, fully created before they stepped onto the stage. They were not performing in extended stage plays where characters may learn and change during the course of two, three, or five acts. In their *entrées* of ten or fifteen minutes, the clowns instantly found their fixed characters in conflict because they could not adjust or cooperate with one another. The three clown musicians could not manage to sit down together, on three separate chairs, at the same time, let alone play music together, until the end of their act. Queenie Moon and Ralph were worlds apart in the kitchen. (Their chicken-cooking *entrée* is printed later.) Queenie Moon and Pino had a problem playing saxophones together. (Pino wanted to play an accordion first.) Pino and Razz found it difficult to dance together as equals. (She was too short and wearing a tux while he was wearing a dress, and so on.)

The Pickle clown acts drew on issues of the day: gender roles, animal rights, and the lost dignity of labor. Geoff Hoyle observes that some comic routines were about "the injustice of the class structure or bureaucracy." "The clowns were underdogs . . . working people in conflict with some authority." This was certainly the case in the *entrée* called *Spaghetti,* where a phone call from the boss throws his employees (the clowns) into a panic. In another *entrée,* Hoyle noted, his clown, Mr. Sniff, took the role of "an annoying authority figure [who is there] like a mosquito" wearing a customs officer's hat, pressuring Willy the Clown to surrender his hat and cane; the conflict turns more grotesque and violent when Sniff saws through Willy's cane and is tempted to saw through poor Willy's leg. (Bill Irwin in his interview observed that the sawing of legs and other limbs was done earlier in the century in a clown act written by Bertolt Brecht; if Brecht's *Baden Learning Play* and its clownish depiction of "man helping man" with a saw blade did not directly influence the Pickles, at least they were aware of it.)

Pino (Diane Wasnak) as a mosquito in *Tossing and Turning*. Photo by David Allen. Courtesy Friends of Olympia Station/New Pickle Circus.

Hoyle was not the only Pickle clown to behave "like a mosquito." In a 1992 circus *entrée*, Diane Wasnak's clown, Pino, portrayed a mosquito complete with comic antennae. Her pestering of an insomniac, the clown Razz, does not constitute the same sort of annoying authority shown by Mr. Sniff; but Razz's battle with a mosquito could be considered a comic tribute to the irrepressible forces of nature. The insect ultimately wins the struggle. Razz, far from a passive victim in the scene, described it this way: "I play the straight man, who wakes up with a mosquito in his bedroom and does everything he can to kill [it]. . . . We pace out like we are having a duel. I see her and do a shooting ducks in a gallery bit to hit the mosquito behind the bed stand. . . . I try a huge flyswatter, which breaks over her head. . . . I spray it with insecticide, which the mosquito likes because it's a mutant. On the blackout, it's cutting me up with a giant knife and fork and sucking my blood with a straw." Wasnak summed up her clown attitude toward her partner here (and toward Queenie Moon in other clown acts), "I love them dearly, but as Pino I just want to irritate the hell out of them."

In another respect, many Pickle clown acts were celebrations of community and cooperation, although they showed the opposite. The clowns would comically replicate, echo, and mock the concept of cooperative collaboration upon which their circus was built. For many years (until the 1990s when shows moved indoors), Pickle company members all worked together to erect canvas walls, move bleachers, and unload their own scenery and costumes. Then in the ring, the clowns would dissolve or parody their everyday cooperation and coordination as they tried to play music or dance together and would fail.

Cooperation returned to the ring at the end of each show. In the finale called *The Big Juggle,* everyone in the circus would come out wearing roustabout costumes and juggle. As cofounder and juggler Peggy Snider said, this juggling act "was the leveler. It was saying to the audience: 'We're really just like you, and we've chosen this path to entertain you. . . . Working together we can help work out this juggling act and a few other things.'"[20] *The Big Juggle* could be regarded as a corrective to the clown acts in which people were unable to accomplish anything or managed to do so only after repeated attempts.

The trio of Irwin, Hoyle, and Pisoni, when they portray musicians, restaurant workers, and furniture movers, resembles a wrecking crew at times; their intense determination and sense of purpose (to play music, serve food, carefully move furniture, dance in unison) are soon derailed by accidents (rehearsed, beautifully timed), acts of mischief, and digressions that leave them at odds with one another, their mission just barely accomplished. Geoff Hoyle said of the popular *entrée The Three Musicians,* "The point had been to sit down and play music; it was that simple." But the simple goal eluded Hoyle, Irwin, and Pisoni's clown trio for twenty to thirty minutes as they kept falling out of chairs, getting stuck in a broken chair, sitting where a chair had been before a partner pulled it away, and tuning up and down.

One could call these comic subversions of shared goals Groucho Marxist tendencies (although Harpo and Chico should not be forgotten here, either). Or, as Joan Mankin said in response to my question about the freedom clowns seek in their acts, "Clowns are anarchistic by nature, and when you've got anarchists—clowns—who are forced to go along with the plot, then you're working against the nature of the clown." Geoff Hoyle noted with some humor that while he and his colleagues "would say the clown acts were about cooperative work, about joyful sharing in attempting an insurmountable task . . . sometimes I think we just said that for the benefit of the grant givers. In fact, we wanted to be as anarchic and outrageous as we could."

These descriptions of clowns as anarchists might be regarded as too confining, too politically charged or reductive by some of the performers (even those I quoted). Still, a more detailed description of anarchism written by one of England's leading anarchists (not a clown, rather a political activist and author), Colin Ward, offers another approach to the dynamics of Pickle clown acts. Developing what he terms "a theory of spontaneous order," Ward writes that "given a common need, a collection of people will, by trial and error, by improvisation and experiment, evolve order out of the situation—this order being more durable and more closely related to their needs than any kind of externally imposed authority could provide."[21]

Could there be a more elegant description of Hoyle, Pisoni, and Irwin in *The Three Musicians,* or of Queenie Moon chasing Electra (Diane

Wasnak), the "demon baby from Hell," who escapes from her carriage, or Razz trying to catch babies (Pino and acrobats in toddlers' clothes) who defiantly bounce off the teeterboard? Yes, there probably could be, but I wanted to introduce Ward's anarchist theory of order anyway. (Yes, there is an anarchist theory of order!) I think clowns who rehearse enough can create acts in which they "spontaneously" arrive at order or equilibrium, after much trial and error, improvisation and experiment, and defying or refusing externally imposed authority. In some cases, though, the Pickle clowns aren't refusing anything; they're simply incapable of cooperating for a while.

A BRIEF PAUSE IN DISEQUILIBRIUM

To arrive at order or equilibrium first requires passage through some disorder, and this journey can be found in almost any Pickle clown act. (Perhaps it is a prerequisite for any clown act, period.) At the risk of introducing another theory that the clowns would mock if given the chance, I want to note French mime Etienne Decroux's writing on the "rebellious articulation" of the body, in which the body moves toward "instability" and, alternately, toward "a brief pause in the disequilibrium through balance."[22] Anyone who saw Hoyle's sausage-nosed clown, Mr. Sniff, balance himself on a stack of teetering chairs before playing the violin, or balance himself on the shoulders of his partner Lorenzo Pickle before playing the violin, with Ms. Wombat seated on Sniff's back playing her violin at the same time, would have a visual sense of how his body moved "through balance" to instability, not quite falling, but nearly.

Hoyle studied mime with Decroux in Paris. I hardly mean to say that Mr. Sniff's rebellious body and instability are Decroux's fault. Nor would I argue that the clowns set out to prove Decroux's theory through their antics. But his theory provides a helpful vocabulary for discussion of their physical comedy. The bodies of the clowns, as they dance, fall, or descend into a circus trunk, move in the ring with a corporeal presence that is hardly theoretical; but their movement is rebellious, at least insofar as their bodies cannot be completely controlled by them or others or find their equilibrium without first resisting its opposite.

Bill Irwin has become rather well known in recent years for a comic dance in which he finds himself drawn toward the wing of a theatre's proscenium arch, as if some huge vacuum is pulling his body in a direction he doesn't want to go. Earlier dances, including some he did for the Pickles, introduced movements that his clown character wanted to retract, or stop, as if, once again, he had lost control of his own body, as if the music had taken over or opposed his freedom of movement, so he took the wrong steps or danced too fast or too far to the left of the stage. It could be that this comic act of lost direction began in his first Pickle Family Circus season, when he was called up to perform an act and, as Irwin notes in his interview, "I didn't have any material. After the circus began its shows, I would often just move as the Pickle band was playing."

At the circus, Mr. Sniff also appeared to lose control of his body when the band played a new dance, "The Boing Boing Boogie Woogie Bounce." He couldn't stop when he wanted, although he was tired, because the band kept playing. The circus announcer didn't have much sympathy for Sniff, either, treating him almost like a bouncing ball. The voice-over said, "Follow the bouncing Mr. Sniff," and urged the audience to sing along while Sniff held up signs with the song title on them.[23] Only when the music stopped could he rest. Hoyle commented that in this act and others, "Sniff is constantly revealing the soft white underbelly, as it were, behind the bravura, the 'magic' behind the trick, as if to say: 'Hey, we're really circus performers, and we're really tired, and you have no idea how hard this is.'" (Other musical acts discussed later, including Hoyle's classic three-legged dance, similarly involved very hard but clownish struggles for secure footing.)

It could be argued that the clowns briefly defy gravity—both seriousness and the laws of physics—through their splendid footwork and balancing acts. (Irwin's post-Pickles performance piece, *The Regard of Flight*, hinted at some interest in life without gravity, even in its title.) The "three-high" balancing act, in which one person stands on the shoulders of another who stands on the shoulders of a third person, gave Hoyle, Pisoni, and Irwin the title of their 1981 winter season of Pickle comedy performed in San Francisco. Of course, they mocked the title terminology by placing mannequins resembling Hoyle and Irwin on Pisoni's shoulders. They took neither gravity nor their defiance of it seriously at that point.

The concept of a "pause" in disequilibrium also deserves a pause. At times, the Pickle clowns reveled in slow takes, repetitions, and extended moments that prolonged their comic conflicts. Both Peggy Snider and Andrea Snow recalled one performance in 1979 when the clowns Sniff and Lorenzo Pickle were extending their act at great length, possibly setting a record, with pauses. At that point, Snow recollected, she and Bill Irwin made an unrehearsed, unannounced entrance as Willy and Ms. Wombat. The two clowns "went out as surveyors and measured the distance between Larry and Geoff, wrote it down on a clipboard, took a couple of other measurements, and left." Mr. Sniff and Lorenzo Pickle "remained perfect statues," although everybody else "was cracking up, the audience and especially the rest of the circus." (The photograph that opens this introduction portrays a tableau close to the one described.) The clown surveyors calculated the "length" of the pause, based on the distance between Lorenzo's and Sniff's noses. (Sniff had a rather long nose to begin with.) Their intervention was a comic tribute to the generous periods of time Pickle clowns enjoyed in the ring. The winners: Sniff and Lorenzo by a nose.

BECKETT'S FRATELLINI

Given all the comic references to physical movement and immobility in Samuel Beckett's plays, I am tempted to call the Pickle clowns post-Beckett comedians. I resist the temptation, because Beckett himself extended physical comedy traditions he encountered in the music hall and in the films of Chaplin, Keaton, and Laurel and Hardy. The Pickle clowns also loved film comedy. There is no single, ultimate source for such behavior, but it is not difficult to imagine the Pickle clowns performing scenes by Beckett. Irwin and Hoyle have performed Beckett's plays to acclaim since leaving the circus. Queenie Moon or Ms. Wombat could provide a superb comic portrayal of Winnie in Beckett's *Happy Days*.

In the circus, the Pickle clown acts sometimes resembled scenes Beckett didn't write but might have. If you take a few lines out of context from

Beckett's *Endgame,* they could serve as dialogue for the three musicians portrayed by Pisoni, Hoyle, and Irwin in the act where they try to seat themselves for a concert. "Is that my place?" "Yes, that's your place." "Am I right in the center?" "More or less! More or less!" "I felt a little too far to the left!" "Now I feel a little too far to the right!" "Now I feel a little too far back."[24] These lines exchanged by Hamm and Clov in Beckett's play, when Hamm's wheelchair is moved, could have been spoken by the three musicians, or by Queenie Moon and Ralph when she narrowly misses hitting him with wooden planks ("A little too far to the left!"), or by Razz as he tries to find the right position on his pillow (portrayed by his partner, Pino, in pillow costume) before falling asleep.

The Pickle clowns did not set out to echo *Endgame* or Beckett's other plays when they created their acts. If I say that they sometimes resemble his characters nonetheless, I mean it as a compliment to them, not as an accusation of derivativeness. Without trying to invoke Beckett's texts, they have given physical form to some of the themes in his plays: in particular, the themes of displacement (exemplified by the tramps on a country road in *Waiting for Godot*) and confinement (what critic Hugh Kenner terms "life in a box," although he is referring to the "box" of the proscenium stage, not a circus storage trunk).[25]

Playwright Jean Anouilh once described *Waiting for Godot* as the "music-hall sketch of Pascal's *Pensées* as played by the Fratellini clowns."[26] The Fratellini never read Pascal, as far as I know; but the Pickle clowns did read Beckett. More important, their own original acts reflect a clown consciousness and physical comedy sensibility contemporary with Beckett's. They could be Beckett's Fratellini. (In interviews, several of the Pickle clowns refer to the Fratellini—although they never claim they wanted to be the Fratellini.)

The many trunk routines performed by Pickle clowns constitute variations on "life in a box." Bill Irwin claims he first started using a trunk because he needed storage space for his props; but his clown, Willy, and Hoyle's Mr. Sniff developed popular acts in which they stepped into trunks and descended out of sight, as if staircases were inside. Lorenzo Pickle often carried a trunk on his back; sometimes it had balloons inside, sometimes other clowns and tubas.

Where Beckett developed grotesque comedy about discarded parents and had Hamm keep his father and mother "bottled up" in trash cans, the Pickle clowns offered more positive, joyous imagery of life in a box. They seemed to thrive in trunks, or at least were willing to step inside, possibly because the circus itself had few walls and they needed privacy once in a while. The descents into their trunks suggested that Willy and Sniff had plenty of room inside.

Perhaps the most intriguing part of Beckett's clown consciousness shared by the Pickles can be seen in their treatment of the ring as a performance space, in which a trunk is just a trunk, without reference to events outside the circus. Bill Irwin speaks of his pleasure in hearing someone say his dance theatre piece, *Largely New York,* could exist only in the theatre. Geoff Hoyle notes that a number of their acts were "about performance. The antagonist is the performance situation itself."

This could be said of Beckett's plays and some of the Pickle clown routines. Their acts are in many ways about self-consciously performing in a specific place and time, the time and place of waiting for Godot to arrive; or for Willy the Clown to catch the spaghetti tossed by Tony the Chef (he keeps missing); or for Sniff and Ms. Wombat to emerge from a trunk (the same trunk) here and now. The trunk is not a second home for these clowns; it is only a trunk. (You can read more into it if you choose, of course. But as Beckett once wrote in his novel *Watt,* "No symbols where none intended.")[27]

The Russian director Meyerhold, who collaborated with clowns several times early in the twentieth century, wrote in his essay on fairground entertainments that "the public comes to the theatre to see the art of man, but what art is there in walking about the stage as oneself?"[28] The Pickle clowns, like other clowns, developed special moves far removed from everyday walking: hat dives, trunk descents, comic walks and dances, leaps, tumbles, stumbles, falls, and flips. Their departure from normal walking and talking distinguishes them as clowns and makes them, if not "surreal," at least nonrealist performers. Their comic walks and dances are inherently critical of normalcy—out of step with the norm—but the steps under consideration here are first of all physical, not economic or political. Economic and social conditions and gender roles affect the acts, too. But sometimes a trunk is just a trunk with a few clowns inside it.

More than "a few"—as many as five clowns—appear to have shared a trunk in one act. *San Francisco Examiner* critic Nancy Scott, who followed the Pickle clown acts for years and loved them, once wrote in an open letter: "I should have preferred a larger number of shorter clown routines because some of them run on longer than they need to, but so much thought and skill has gone into each one that it's ungrateful to complain, and who would not be tickled with the routine in which the clown who looks like a duck in a slicker (Geoff Hoyle) multiplies into four identical ducks in slickers to the mystification of Pisoni who thought he had the fellow safely shut up in a trunk. The choreography of that one would tax the San Francisco ballet."[29]

The act to which she refers, sometimes known as *Multiple Sniffs*, was choreographed by Kimi Okada, and it placed in the ring between four and seven Mr. Sniffs who defied Lorenzo Pickle's efforts to keep them, and the circus, under his control, locked in a box. If an act with clowns who refuse to stay inside a trunk had been performed in Russia during much of the past century, Western critics might have heralded it as a daring parable about resistance to Soviet authority. In San Francisco, it was not just another trunk act, either. As Hoyle said of the act: "In the ring, everything is possible; yes, you can put people in trunks. And people can pop out of them. It's a metaphor." But in San Francisco, the metaphorical and metacomic implications of an irrepressible impulse toward freedom from confinement, exercised by a clown who keeps coming back in multiplied numbers, were understated if not unseen, like all those Sniffs hidden in a trunk. (The eastern European critic Ernst Fischer once noted that Beckett's *Endgame* is a play about confinement, too, and he compared it to a Solzhenitsyn novel about prison life.[30] Beckett's plays were prohibited from performance in Moscow until the openness of *glasnost* arrived in the 1980s. But few critics would argue that Beckett set out to write a play about prison.)

The Russian clowns Leonid Yengebarov and Anatoly Marchevsky (both coached by Yuri Belov, who is currently living in San Francisco) used to refuse to leave the ring when a ringmaster or his assistant tried to get them off and bring on another act. Their refusals to cooperate, to fit in and not to delay or interrupt the program, have counterparts in Pickle Family acts where the clowns stay onstage ("longer than they need to," as Scott said), failing to cooperate with one another for long periods. But none of the Pickle clowns performed in Moscow during its Soviet Communist period, where and when their antiauthoritarian tendencies might have been more clearly seen as such. In the current free-market Moscow, their trunk acts could be seen differently, as parables about possessive, acquisitive societies. In any event, the trunk acts have mostly been put in storage or moved with their owners out of the Pickles to other venues like Irwin's *Fool Moon* on Broadway.

By 1988, after Mr. Sniff, Willy, and Lorenzo Pickle had departed from the Pickle Family Circus, trunks and Beckettian comedy were less likely to be seen in the ring. The circus moved in a new direction where separate acts became part of a larger story. In *Café des Artistes* (1988–1989), *La La Luna Sea* (1990), *Tossing and Turning* (1992), and *Jump Cuts!* (1994), the clowns retained distinctive identities, but instead of fitting into a trunk, they had to fit into a new structure: a circus narrative.

THE CIRCUS OF THE FUTURE?

Whenever clowns discuss the circus of the future, they are likely to refer to Cirque du Soleil and its integration of diverse acts into a larger narrative. This tendency, which has been popularized by the Canadian Cirque, could be seen in Pickle Family Circus acts around the same time it emerged in Montreal, in the late 1980s. Which circus first perfected the form can be debated; I would say neither of them perfected it, at least as far as clown acts are involved, because it reduces the independence (anarchism, if you will) of action inherent in clowning.

Ironically, the first of these "future circus" presentations created by the Pickles was inspired by an old turn-of-the-century vaudeville act. Judy Finelli, artistic director of the Pickle Family Circus in 1989, said she drew on the vaudeville act *An Animated Supper Chez Maxim's*, in which each performer portrayed "a different character, they were in a restaurant, and they did their specialities.... At the end, they were in a semicircle, one guy caught all the plates, one at a time, and fell over."[31] Under Finelli's direction, the Pickles revived this scenario, with variations to suit their own specialty acts. The result was an hour-long act titled *Café des Artistes;* its action concerned a group of café workers and customers, all of whom turn out to have gifts as circus performers. Where some cafés serve as meeting places for artists, this one became a performance arena. Characters displayed their traits primarily through juggling, balancing, and a trapeze act. *La La Luna Sea,* the next narrative Pickle Family Circus presentation, featured the clowns Queenie Moon and Pino in 1990. Their action was more central to the scenario. Joan Mankin noted that they were able to perform the equivalent of an *entrée* early in the story, as they toyed with a piano onstage. Later Pickle presentations with narrative also gave the clowns Pino and Razz more opportunities for *entrées.*

In my discussions about narrative circus with different clowns, I heard different responses. Larry Pisoni thought that "when you interject plot into a circus performance, it often slows the whole thing down, because you need time for exposition, and you need time to establish character." Jeff Raz and Diane Wasnak, able to create their own acts in a narrative for the New Pickle Circus, felt involved and pleased with the artistic achievements.

Raz quite perceptively suggested that the best narrative form in his experience, the 1992 *Tossing and Turning,* had more in common with dance or dance theatre than with narrative theatre. This is not surprising, since circus director Tandy Beal is also a dance choreographer. Her production of *Tossing and Turning* portrays the nightlife of an insomniac, Razz, full of surreal and comic episodes, linked by failed efforts of the clown to fall asleep. Razz's partner Pino keeps him awake much of the time with a series of incursions on his repose. Dressed as his pillow in one scene, a mosquito in another, Pino won't let the man sleep. The actions don't have a terribly complex narrative structure. Tandy Beal said the presentation was "not strict narrative" but rather a sequence of images and metaphors inspired by the topic of insomnia. That inspiration was enough to give the diverse acts a quirky, dreamlike coherence. Accompanied by music throughout, the evening crossed boundaries between dance, circus, and theatre. The clown acts could have stood on their own, but they acquired additional resonance as part of an increasingly preposterous sequence of sleep disruptions. Raz also noted that this production "put the clowns in the wonderful position of being the storytellers, being the connective tissue."

Joan Mankin had some reservations about clowning in *La La Luna Sea*. She noted that "although Diane [Wasnak] and I were the protagonist and antagonist of the piece . . . in another sense we were merely clowns in a much larger picture." The sense that Pino and Queenie were "merely clowns" may have been shared by the audience, as their clown acts were less distinctive and less outrageous than they had been in self-contained acts, such as one in which Wasnak portrays Electra, the demon baby from hell, and Queenie tries to get the escaped baby back in her carriage. Mankin felt that "the best clowning comes when you don't have to follow a line. You can go where you want to go . . . and not have to be faithful to a narrative."

The future popularity of narrative circus is more likely to be determined by Cirque du Soleil than the Pickles, if only because Cirque is larger, far wealthier, and more widely seen through its tours and multiple shows. Geoff Hoyle, who performed as a clown with Cirque du Soleil for one season, felt "the most recent Cirque du Soleil shows' narratives are so vague and abstract, they become to my mind almost pretentious. 'It is about everything, because it is about nothing.' I would agree with Mr. Sniff: 'If it's about nothing, it's about nothing.'"

The fact that seven Pickle artists (not clowns) joined Cirque du Soleil in 1998 raises another question about the future of the Pickle circus: Can artists afford not to run away to the Cirque when it offers an attractive contract?

THE RETURN OF THE MILLIONAIRE TRAMP

The torn, shabby costume of the clown tramp that Charlie Chaplin and Emmett Kelly popularized in the United States initially reflected the poverty of struggling performers, as well as that of the homeless and unemployed civilians who had to wear such clothing. In an old, torn tuxedo and slightly smashed top hat, a clown might also resemble a formerly wealthy citizen who met hard times. Chaplin dreamed of portraying such a "millionaire tramp" early in his career, years before the "Little Tramp" became popular enough to make Chaplin himself a millionaire.[32]

While the Pickle clowns have worn their share of old top hats and less-than-elegant evening clothes, they rarely performed *entrées* about former millionaires, wealth, and poverty. One exception is *Spaghetti,* the routine in which Irwin and Hoyle have a short dialogue about their status as wage slaves:

> *Willy (Irwin):* Tony, I hope you told the Boss that I'm a tired to be a wage slave.
> *Tony (Hoyle):* Si, Willy, si.
> *Willy:* What he say?
> *Tony:* No more wages. . . . Now we worken on a commission.
> *Willy:* What a means commission?
> *Tony:* No customers, no pay.

The two clowns, waiter and chef, would then find a customer and, desperate to please after they had run out of spaghetti, offer a pie, usually placed in one of their own faces. It brought them applause and laughter, which meant they were fulfilling their jobs as clowns if not as food servers.

These jokes, created early in Pickle Family Circus history, proved to be slightly prophetic, since the clowns did cease to be "wage slaves" and needed "commissions" at a certain point. Initially, a number of them (Irwin, Pisoni, Hoyle) were paid a living wage by the Comprehensive Employment and Training Act (CETA). During their first years with the circus, they hardly became rich from these wages, but CETA grants represented a small government subsidy. The steady income permitted them to continue comic collaborations both at the circus and in public schools. In San Francisco schools, as Irwin noted, the clowns could engage in "pure clowning."[33] Removed from other circus obligations, they shared new clown acts with diverse young audiences in a show they called *Vinegar* and had extra time to practice their art.

CETA support ended toward the end of 1979, a year when seven of the twenty members of the Pickle Family Circus held CETA-funded positions.

(Three were performers; one was the musical director; one, the technical director; one, the assistant business manager; and one, the publicist–tour booker.) Like the restaurant clowns in *Spaghetti*, the circus itself became more dependent on "commission," including Arts Commission grants, National Endowment for the Arts grants, and ticket sales.

The only American precedent for federal wages paid to circus artists prior to CETA was the Federal Theatre Project (FTP) of the Works Progress Administration in the 1930s. The Federal Theatre Project paid performers of vaudeville acts, dances, stage plays, puppetry, and a circus in New York with dozens of clowns. The low wages allowed FTP and CETA artists to develop their talents. If acts by the Pickle clowns were relatively free from discussion of money, it may have been because the government briefly—and only partially—freed them from commercial pressures, and their artistry thrived.

Looking back on that period, Irwin recalled, "It was not always easy. The CETA program came about because there was a recession. So there was always the question: 'God, this profession! Is there really a living to be made?'" He and most of the other Pickle clowns have continued to make a living through comic performance, but to do so they have worked in other circuses, theatres, films, dance concerts, and solo shows, even for the Disney corporation.

The Pickle clowns have left the circus in search of new and different artistic challenges, as well as higher income. Clown-centered as the Pickle circus was, the *entrées* usually lasted only fifteen or twenty minutes; the clowns were able to develop more complex, longer shows elsewhere. *Three High*, the evening of short plays created by Pisoni, Hoyle, Irwin, and friends in 1981, was one endeavor to move their circus clowning, along with acting and comic writing, into a theatre space. As Larry Pisoni notes: "The three of us had seen some limitations to the outdoor show. We wanted more control of the environment. All of the clown material in the circus was written for a mixed audience (adults and children). I had a desire to write and perform material in a venue that was specifically for adults."

Jazz saxophonist and circus band musician Harvey Robb, who also participated in *Three High*, observed that the work of all the artists involved in the stage project "pushed things to another level, with added risk and added expense in going 'downtown.'"[34] They were taken more seriously, by themselves and others, when they moved out of the circus ring; a move into a proscenium theatre allowed them to be seen as actors and writers. Since then, they have continued to demonstrate their versatility, but that required leaving the circus. Geoff Hoyle, who won great acclaim for the lead role in Dario Fo's satire *Accidental Death of an Anarchist,* directed by Tony Taccone at San Francisco's Eureka Theatre, said that when "I did [that play], I felt that I was proving to the theatre community that I could work in a play, that I could not 'just be a clown.'" He added that some of his best clowning occurs when he is acting in a play, and in that sense, he has not left one profession for another.

The Pickle Family Circus itself moved on, or moved into another phase of its career, in 1993 when it went bankrupt and was reorganized as the New Pickle Circus. Even before the bankruptcy, the group had reorganized in some respects. Cofounder and artistic director Larry Pisoni left in 1987, and Judy Finelli, his former juggling partner, took charge. The touring practices through which the company saved money—by performing outdoors and having artists camp in tents—began to change, too. By the late 1980s, the equipment had become heavier, and performances moved indoors. The tour circuit changed, as old sites were no longer suitable; and some audience and community support was lost in the shift. In an account of this crisis published in the June 1993 *Callboard,* Diana Scott notes that "the move indoors entailed, along with the need to build new audiences, unprecedented expenses: hotel bills . . . per diems . . . technical expenses . . . not to mention theatre rental and pre-production costs."[35]

The clowns were affected by these changes, but not entirely for the worse. Diane Wasnak said that during the tour of *La La Luna Sea* in 1990, "everybody was in everything. I was doing teeterboard, pole climbing, hoop diving, playing music, doing word stuff. I was on the rigging crew. I was onstage the entire time except for intermission, in a two-hour show twice a day, sometimes outside in 100-plus degree weather. I couldn't do that now. It wasn't as much work when *Luna Sea* was performed indoors." (The excessive workload here also could be attributed to the size of the company and the budget; both were too small for a show like *La La Luna Sea.*)

While the performers were freed from some physical labors after the circus moved indoors and they no longer had to set up bleachers, light poles, or sidewalls, they also were no longer the circus "family" and cooperative of Pisoni's era. As Diana Scott observed, Larry Pisoni "built the Pickle Family Circus on a family model of circus culture, in which everyone does a bit of everything—all members have all skills. This culture is supported by miles traveled together, trailers lived in, family lived with, and cannot be replaced, even with an extraordinary teacher."[36]

Although the "family" could not be replaced by a teacher, a circus school had opened in 1983 under Pickle auspices, with Wendy Parkman and Judy Finelli's direction. Variations of that first circus school continue in San Francisco, but until recently there were few clowning classes in the school. This situation could change in the future; in spring of 2000, the National Endowment for the Arts awarded the San Francisco School of Circus Arts a grant to support the training of clowns. The timing of the award was particularly interesting, since Ringling Bros. had closed its educational program known as Clown College a year earlier.

In recent times, the temptation to run away from the circus, or at least leave the Pickles for another circus, has led some artists to join Cirque du Soleil, as already noted. Besides Geoff Hoyle, who spent one season as a featured clown with Cirque, Diane Wasnak clowned in their Las Vegas show. Pickle artists John Gilkey, Lorenzo Pisoni, and Gypsy Snider (the latter two the children of circus founders Larry Pisoni and Peggy Snider) have also been featured in Cirque du Soleil. Tandy Beal told me that the New Pickle Circus artists who joined a Cirque du Soleil show in 1998 "call themselves 'The San Francisco Seven.'" While these artists will not become millionaires in Cirque, either, there is no question that the prospects of higher pay in a large, popular circus company attracted some of them. Beal added: "We can't afford to keep training people just so they come to the level that Cirque will want."

Although it did not set out to be a learning center, the Pickle circus, together with the circus school founded by Pickle artists, has proven to be a wonderful training ground for clowns and other circus artists. Jack Golden, who joined the Pickles with the understanding he would stay only one year and who performed as the clown Poot with his partner, Sharon Ostreicher ("Moxie" in the ring), during the 1985 circus season, told me that his time with the circus gave him a great education: "The year with the circus was a significant part of my career. It taught me how to be a performer. . . . For other circuses you have to be established already to get the part, even to audition for the part. I'm not the first person who came to the Pickles saying, 'I've never done this before.' . . . It was an arena that fostered young performers."[37]

Another Pickle performer, Derique McGee, was attracted to the Pickles because he wanted to be a clown. In his three years with the circus (1982–1984), he did not become a featured clown; he appeared in juggling and acrobatic acts and as a member of the gorilla chorus line. But McGee, who now earns his living as a clown and tours his own shows, says he "learned a lot about clowning from Larry Pisoni." He watched Pisoni for three years, "and he [Pisoni] directed some of my own clown pieces, while I was with the Pickles and in the 1987 New Vaudeville Festival." While he was with the Pickles, McGee also earned a B.A. degree in circus arts and physical comedy at New College of California. The circus was literally part of his independent study program in college; or, as McGee says about his double life as student and circus artist, "I got a two-for-one."[38]

In 2000, the San Francisco School of Circus Arts created another form of two-for-one as it officially purchased and became owner of the New Pickle Circus. (Prior to that, the two were financially separate entities.) If the Pickle clowns do not constitute a school, at least they now have a school. But they always have been well educated. For a quarter of a century, the Pickle circus offered its artists a small but intimate venue in which to develop new acts and grow artistically with encouragement from the director and colleagues. Unlike larger circuses, where comic artists might be lost, squeezed between main events in three rings, the Pickle clowns have been given time and the center of attention in the ring. Their circus cannot compete with Cirque du Soleil's high finances and high-tech spectacle, but that may be for the best, if the Pickle circus is to remain, in Beal's words, "human-sized." I think that is how Larry Pisoni saw it when he founded the circus to celebrate "human experience and healthy relationships," and that continued to be one of its greatest strengths.

Geoff Hoyle provides a wonderful story about the difference between the human-sized Pickle circus and the high-tech clowning of Cirque du Soleil. When Hoyle was Mr. Sniff in the Pickle Family Circus, he collaborated with percussionist Keith Terry to create a funny sound effect. Sniff's long sausage-nosed sniffing could be heard every time Terry rubbed the top of an oatmeal box in front of a microphone; through practice, the clown and the musician were able to coordinate their timing perfectly for this comic effect. When Hoyle was a guest with Cirque du Soleil, the sound effect was recorded. A button was pushed, and the nose-sniffing would be heard on an electronic synthesizer; however, "the synthesizer never worked," says Hoyle. The prerecorded, push-button sound was far less precise than musician Terry. Human comedy proved superior to machine-assisted clowning. For those who don't want to be technologically advanced wage slaves (for high wages) with Cirque, the Pickle circus's simplicity, relatively low tech and with a resourceful live band, may still hold attractions.

THE TRIUMPH OF THE ECCENTRIC

In their "human-sized" circus artistry, the Pickle clowns sometimes parody the largest of American spectacles: Hollywood and Broadway are paid homage and reduced to clownery at the same time in a number of eccentric dances.

One clown act Pino and Razz first developed in 1994 for *Jump Cuts!*, and revived in 1998, was titled *Let's Face the Music and* . . . Their pseudoromantic dance recalled numbers popularized by Fred Astaire and Ginger Rogers, only in this instance, Razz, the man, wore the strapless gown and Pino wore a silver tux. She climbed up a ladder to reach her partner's height. Their reversal of roles, and vertical differences, suggested the match was far from Hollywood's standards of perfection.

When gorillas danced in a chorus line for the Pickles in an earlier season, that too, as Kimi Okada noted, "ended up as a goof on a big show-biz, show-stopping dance." In 1992, Tandy Beal choreographed a dance parade for a human-sized tomato sandwich, complete with a piece of cheese and a pickle, in *Tossing and Turning*. It was, as far as I know, the first time a performer in a pickle costume danced in the Pickle circus.

Another comic dance, which can be seen in the 1978 video *It's the Pickle Family Circus,* opens with Willy the Clown dancing his welcome to the audience.[39] Bill Irwin as Willy enters looking like a cross between a tramp millionaire and a Kabuki actor, with black lips and black vertical lines above and below his eyes over white face paint. Dressed in a black top hat, tuxedo, orange-red wig, and dark-red bulb of a nose, Willy is too elegant for the warm summer afternoon on which he performs outdoors. Parents and children in the audience sit in front of him wearing shorts, slacks, T-shirts. The clown looks incongruously formal in the setting; he is an eccentric even before he starts to dance.

Phil Marsh sings his lyrics, "Presenting Willy the Clown," the band music plays, and Willy spreads his arms out wide, ready to take flight or preserve his balance. He crouches slightly, swivels arms and hips, waddles in a circle, gyrates his white-gloved hands, and adds some chicken-wing elbow action. Suddenly, with no fanfare, Willy drops his top hat on the ground. It lands brim up, and he dives head-first into the top hat, somersaults, lands in a split with his head bowed over his extended right leg, hat on head. His small but spectacular feat recalls another kind of open-air act: the legendary dive a fairground rider on a white horse used to take from a high tower into a water barrel. Willy's dive is much more daring—into a container smaller than a barrel, with no water to cushion his impact.

These comic movements to music in Pickle clown *entrées* continue, with variation, the American vaudeville tradition known as "eccentric dance." Joe Laurie Jr., in his book *Vaudeville,* calls eccentric dancers "the Edisons of hoofology" and counts among them Ray Bolger, Harlan Dixon, Martha Raye, Ben Blue, Bert Williams, Eddie Foy Jr., Fanny Brice, Leon Errol, Will Mahoney, and Jack Donohue.[40] In vaudeville, Bolger was given the first name "Rubberlegs." Leon Errol was famous for a rubber-legged drunken step. Will Mahoney had small hammers attached to his feet and played a xylophone by dancing on it. Fanny Brice was acclaimed for her comic dance of 1939 entitled "Dying Swan Ballet." Lotte Goslar, although not a vaudevillian, developed her own repertoire of eccentric dances in Germany and America between the 1930s and 1990s; her ensemble, Lotte Goslar's Pantomime Circus, performed these numbers with her. (Another form of eccentric circus performance has surfaced in recent years among American groups like the Bindlestiff Family Cirkus, Circus Amok, and Coney Island USA; their adventurous new acts with bearded ladies, fire eaters, and sword swallowers draw more on the traditions of sideshow eccentricity and punk rock than on vaudevillian dance.)

The Pickle clowns have not become famous as eccentric dancers, and except for some of Irwin's parodies of postmodern dance and break dancing and for Hoyle's three-legged dance and *Out of the Inkwell*, done after Irwin and Hoyle left the Pickles, they hardly rival the vaudeville era's hoofers. However, it could be argued that in the pratfalls, rolls, and other acrobatic moves the Pickle clowns perform to live musical accompaniment, their acts approach the seemingly drunken, rubber-legged movements of Bolger and Errol, who were not drunk but superbly in control of their bodies. As Tandy Beal noted in her discussion of clowns and dancers, both groups depend on their sense of timing "to find the right moment," for either the jeté or the joke. Leap and joke could occur at the same time in an eccentric circus dance.

Kimi Okada, who choreographed superb comic dance for Robin Williams, as well as for Irwin, Hoyle, Pisoni, and other Pickles, noted that in such work, a strong sense of character is required. The humor is connected to "character, emotion, a situation which is innately funny, or is a setup to be funny." Trained dancers without the comic character of a clown could not achieve the same effect. Willy the Clown deprived of his name, distinctive nervous swivels, red hair, formal attire, and special makeup might just be another dancer diving into a top hat.

More than a body or bodies in disequilibrium are needed here; comic characters as fully formed as the Pickle clowns were before the music started contributed to a comic relationship among them in their dances and to the highly stylized acting in their *entrées*. Willy with his nervousness and ineptitude, Mr. Sniff with his overdependence on olfactory sensitivity, Pino with her annoying persistence (or persisting annoyance) step out with an attitude.

If the clowns are out of step, unable to dance in unison (as was the case with Hoyle, Pisoni, and Irwin in their *Reunion Dance*), or unable to dance like Astaire and Rogers, or to sit down in concert in their concert chairs, it is due at least in part to their comic characters, clownish fears, obstinacy, and practiced miscalculation that cause things to go wrong at just the right time. Geoff Hoyle suggested that "the tyranny of things" like broken chairs may contribute to their failings; but in the end, if the clowns want to sit down and play music, and if comically unstoppable determination is part of their characters (it is), then broken chairs will not stop them.

When they danced solo—Hoyle with his three legs, Irwin with his body mysteriously drawn toward stage left—each character had to adjust to his own legs (instead of chairs or fellow clowns), as if the legs had become independent from other parts of him. This variation on eccentric dance was closer to the original vaudevillian impulse to dance like crazy, even if the legs do not always agree with the upper torso or the music about which way to go.

Clown characters are not like the personae developed by most actors and dancers. As Andrea Snow noted in her interview, "Some 'great [authority]' . . . said it takes nine months [for an actor] to perfect a role. It must take years to perfect a clown character. . . . My guess is that he or she can go very deep investigating the particular tendency or excess or essential thing his [or her] clown is." The depth is not one of psychological complexity but rather a complexity of physical behavior, of which eccentric dance is one manifestation. You don't have to be a dancer to be eccentric, however, particularly when you're a Pickle clown.

In fact, *not* dancing is the eccentric act in one number. The gorillas try to be dainty and precise as they prance across the Pickle Family Circus ring and force the one human figure (the clown Lorenzo Pickle) to follow their lead. As Larry Pisoni recalled it, his character is "terrorized by these apes . . . [and finds that] the one way he can survive and thrive is to dance with them. Not only does he dance with them, but he's enjoying the dance." His movements copy theirs, and gradually he begins to relax. His resistance disappears, and you can see it in his body, as he sways with the rest of the gang.

After Lorenzo Pickle adopts the gorillas' behavior, we see a new society of sorts, a clown-gorilla collaboration that ends in the construction of a pyramid. It can't be called a "human pyramid," because a clown and gorillas compose it. (Sara Felder, a juggler who performed as one of the dancing gorillas, recalls the humorous scene backstage: costumed dancers needing fresh air would often hold gorilla heads in their hands—everyone was part human, part gorilla at that point.[41]) The pyramid composed of clown and dancing gorillas stands as a living monument to the eccentric. By definition, eccentrics are supposed to be off-center. Here, in a celebration of difference and diversity, among gorillas and others, we see an eccentric in the center, as he should be in a circus where clowns run the show.

My earlier reference to the Pickle clowns as "Fratellini American" was not quite accurate. Given the Pickle clowns' affinity with the eccentrics of

The gorilla chorus line with Lorenzo Pickle (Larry Pisoni). Photo by Terry Lorant.

vaudeville and the fact that the Pickles include too many women clowns to be brothers (as Paul, Albert, and François Fratellini were), it is misleading to suggest the Pickles are the new Fratellini. Their family is too American and too diverse for that. Still, their "clown utopia" represents an important American variation of the European circus in which comic artists are celebrated for their *entrées* and are given a ring in which to perform complete small plays. Their creativity has been freed from the restrictions that variety show formats and narrative sequences often impose on circus artists. Rather than working as auxiliaries to other, more prominent acts, or adapting their work to fit between featured acts, the Pickle clowns have been the center of attention in their circus; and after they leave the circus, they remain at the center—as welcome eccentrics—wherever they go.

NOTES

1. Benjamin, "The Work of Art in the Age of Mechanical Reproduction," 231.

2. Carol Pogash, "A New Big Tent in the Mission," *San Francisco Examiner,* May 10, 1975, p. 1.

3. The Fratellini trio, composed of the brothers Paul, François, and Albert, became enormously popular in Paris in the 1920s. Besides performing their own *entrées* at Cirque Medrano and Cirque d'Hiver, they were featured in Jean Cocteau's play *Le Boeuf sur le Toit* and served as teachers in director Jacques Copeau's theatre school, Le Vieux Colombier. Paul was the *auguste* clown, his character not terribly bright, usually dressed in a shabby suit, monocle, and top hat. François, elegantly clothed in satin, was the clever whiteface clown. Albert was the *contre-auguste*—the wild card who wore a bulbous red nose and variously colored wigs and was the frequent target of his brothers' schemes. (He was literally the target in one *entrée* titled *William Tell,* where François tried to shoot an apple placed on top of Albert's head; but Albert ate the apple instead.)

Traditional circus *entrées* involved a scenario in which the *auguste* suffered a beating or loss of dignity from the whiteface. The Fratellini acts often had two clown characters (Paul and François) team up against the *contre-auguste,* Albert.

In comparing Hoyle, Pisoni, and Irwin to the Fratellini, I do not mean to suggest that each of the three Pickles played one of the Fratellini roles, only that the Pickles also performed *entrées* as a trio and did so masterfully. The San Francisco clowns were not copying the Fratellini, as they learned from diverse traditions and acts and developed their own original characteristics. As I note toward the end of my introduction, it is slightly inaccurate to call the Pickle trio "Fratellini American." And yet, few if any other modern American circuses had a trio that could provoke such comparisons to the Fratellini. New York's Big Apple Circus in the 1980s deserves acknowledgment in this context, too, for its trio of Stubs (Michael Christensen), Gordoon (Jeff Gordon), and Grandma (Barry Lubin).

Kenneth Little has attributed a decline in the popularity of the circus *entrée* to the fact that in recent times, clowning "has found its way into the circus ring from the streets, from folk and mime festivals, the theatre, and clown schools throughout Europe. And, while it has not replaced the traditional clown entree [*sic*] altogether . . . [the new] comic style is not that of the entree form. It is variously referred to as Clown Art, Clown-Miming, or Theatre Clowning. In the United States, such clowns are known as the New Vaudevillians, Postmodern Clowns, or New Wave Comics" (Little 55). While I would not call the Pickle clowns "New Vaudevillians, Postmodern Clowns, or New Wave Comics," I am inclined to agree with Little's thesis that in recent years, clowns, including the Pickles (whom he does not discuss), have learned from diverse practices of comedy, not only from the traditional *entrée* roles of *auguste* and whiteface clown. At the same time, I would argue that the Pickle clowns in their own way have renewed and adopted the traditional European *entrée* and shown that small plays complete with comic characters and dialogue can be popular in an American circus.

4. Lu Yi trained and rehearsed with many Pickle circus artists prior to his appointment as artistic director of the New Pickle Circus in 2000. He began teaching acrobatics at the San Francisco School of Circus Arts in 1990 after his arrival from China. He previously performed with the Shanghai Red Acrobatic Troupe and the Nanjing Acrobatics Troupe; his acts included plate spinning, martial arts, and "pagoda of bowls." He also served as a trainer with Circus Oz in Australia and at the Big Apple Circus in New York and was artistic director of the Nanjing Acrobatics Troupe. In December 1999, he directed *Yu San* (Harmony), a circus performance featuring Pickle circus artists and School of Circus Arts students. Discussing the training of circus artists, he told me that "many people who begin their study here don't know exactly what acrobats are. They think that circus is where you juggle, clown, or work with animals. For me, circus involves use of the body to perform different acts and different skills; we use the body for handstands, the teeterboard, the trapeze, contortions, juggling" (conversation on November 18, 1999).

5. Dan Rice lived from 1823 to 1900. Besides parodying Shakespeare, he developed a clown character who looked like Uncle Sam and ran for the office of president of the United States in 1868. He lost the race and eventually returned to the circus world. Rice delivered comic monologues in the ring and engaged in humorous dialogue with his circus's ringmaster.

6. Peggy Snider in conversations with the author, San Francisco, November 18, 1998.

7. Joan Mankin interview. Unless otherwise noted, all quotations from the Pickle clowns are taken from the interviews included in this book.

8. Jeffrey Gaeto in Carroll and Lorant, *The Pickle Family Circus*, 95.

9. Carroll, "San Francisco's Pickle Family Circus," 3.

10. Albrecht, *The New American Circus,* 29–30.

11. Robert Hurwitt, "A Pickle for Your Thoughts," *East Bay Express* (Berkeley), May 13, 1988, p. 23, and "Pickle Circus Is a Gem This Year," *San Francisco Examiner,* December 14, 1992, p. B2.

12. Sources for quotations: Robert Hurwitt, "A Sweet Pickles Story," *San Francisco Examiner,* October 22, 1993, p. D7; Tandy Beal in conversation with the author; Nancy Scott, *San Francisco Examiner,* "There's a new brand of Pickles, but don't be jarred," May 6, 1988, p. C1; Harry McFarland, *Daily News* (Ketchikan, Alaska), August 1979; Doris Lessing, back cover of Carroll and Lorant, *The Pickle Family Circus;* Robert Hurwitt, "A Pickle for Your Thoughts," p. 23; unsigned article, *San Jose Mercury News,* June 3, 1979.

13. Alfred Frankenstein, "An Imaginative Delight," *San Francisco Chronicle,* July 7, 1976, p. 45.

14. Jenkins, *Acrobats of the Soul,* 120–21.

15. Del Monte Pickle advertisement in program for the 1987 season of the Pickle Family Circus, p. 8.

16. May, *The Circus from Rome to Ringling,* 303–4.

17. Judy Finelli in conversation with the author, San Francisco, November 25, 1998.

18. Jacob, *Arts du Cirque.*

19. Snider in conversation with the author, San Francisco, November 28, 1998.

20. Snider in conversation with the author, San Francisco, November 28, 1998.

21. Ward, *Anarchy in Action,* 28.

22. Decroux, *Words on Mime,* 69, 81.

23. Source is *It's the Pickle Family Circus* videocassette.

24. Beckett, *Endgame,* 26–27.

25. Kenner, *Samuel Beckett,* 133.

26. Anouilh, "*Godot* or the Music-Hall Sketch of Pascal's *Pensées* as Played by the Fratellini Clowns," 12–13.

27. Beckett, *Watt,* 254.

28. Meyerhold, "The Fairground Booth," 130.

29. Nancy Scott, "A Love Letter to the Pickle Family Circus," *San Francisco Examiner,* May 14, 1981, p. E6.

30. Fischer, *Art Against Ideology.*

31. Finelli in conversation with the author, San Francisco, November 25, 1998.

32. Chaplin, *My Autobiography,* 37.

33. San Francisco was the first city to use CETA funds for performing and visual artists and teachers, according to Jo Sonn in the journal *CETAlaska* (September 1970): 8.

34. Harvey Robb in conversation with the author, San Francisco, November 17, 1998.

35. Scott, "Bang the Drum Slowly," 5.

36. Scott, "Bang the Drum Slowly," 6.

37. Jack Golden in conversation with the author, San Francisco, December 12, 1998.

38. Derique McGee in conversation with the author, San Francisco, January 21, 1999.

It also should be noted that Cecil MacKinnon, a former Pickle juggler and acrobat, has achieved distinction as the clown Yo-Yo with Circus Flora. She acquired some experience in clowning with the Pickles, as she performed comic acts with Hoyle, Irwin, and Pisoni, notably their *Ace Moving Men* number, in which she played the role of a widow, and she engaged in comic acrobatics with an ensemble the Pickles called "The Flying Linguini."

39. Source is *It's the Pickle Family Circus* videocassette.

40. Laurie, *Vaudeville*, 46–47.

41. Sara Felder in conversation with the author, San Francisco, February 14, 1999.

BIBLIOGRAPHY

Albrecht, Ernest. *The New American Circus.* Gainesville: University Press of Florida, 1995.

Anouilh, Jean. "*Godot* or the Music-Hall Sketch of Pascal's *Pensées* as Played by the Fratellini Clowns." In *Casebook on* Waiting for Godot, translated and edited by Ruby Cohn, 12–13. New York: Grove Press, 1967.

Beckett, Samuel. *Endgame.* New York: Grove Press, 1958.

———. *Watt.* New York: Grove Press, 1959.

Benjamin, Walter. "The Work of Art in the Age of Mechanical Reproduction." In *Illuminations,* translated by Harry Zohn. New York: Schocken, 1973.

Carroll, Jon. "San Francisco's Pickle Family Circus." Program notes for *Pickle Clown Reunion.* San Francisco, October 25–26, 1985.

Carroll, Jon, and Terry Lorant. *The Pickle Family Circus.* San Francisco: Chronicle Books, 1986.

Chaplin, Charles. *My Autobiography.* New York: Pocket Books, 1966.

Cooper, Diana Starr. *Night after Night.* Washington, D.C.: Island Press, 1994.

Decroux, Etienne. *Words on Mime.* Translated by Mark Piper. Claremont, Calif.: *Mime Journal,* 1985.

Fischer, Ernst. *Art Against Ideology.* New York: Braziller, 1969.

Fratellini, Albert. *Nous, Les Fratellini.* Paris: Grasset, 1955.

Grimaldi, Joseph. *Memoirs of Joseph Grimaldi.* Edited by Boz [Charles Dickens]. London: Routledge, 1838. Reprint, c. 1880.

Gussow, Mel. "Profiles: Clown" [Bill Irwin]. *New Yorker,* Nov. 11, 1985, 51–87.

It's the Pickle Family Circus. Directed by Steve Christensen and Jim Mayer. 29 min. Woodland Video, 1978. Videocassette.

Jacob, Pascal. *Arts du Cirque.* Pamphlet. Chalons en Champagne, France, 1995.

Jenkins, Ron. *Acrobats of the Soul.* New York: TCG, 1988.

Kenner, Hugh. *Samuel Beckett.* London: Calder, 1962.

Laurie, Joe, Jr. *Vaudeville.* New York: Henry Holt, 1953.

Little, Kenneth. "Pitu's Doubt: Entree Clown Self-Fashioning in the Circus Tradition." *Drama Review* 30.4 (winter 1986): 55.

May, Earl Chapin. *The Circus from Rome to Ringling.* New York: Dover, 1963.

Mayhew, Henry. *London Labour and the London Poor, Volume III.* 1861. Reprint, New York: Dover, 1968.

Meyerhold, Vsevelod. "The Fairground Booth." In *Meyerhold on Theatre,* translated and edited by Edward Braun. New York: Hill and Wang, 1969.

Putting Up the Pickles. Directed by Carrie and Yasha Aginsky. 30 min. Direct Cinema, Ltd., 1981. Videocassette.

Rémy, Tristan. *Les Clowns.* Paris: Grasset, 1945.

———. *Clowns Scenes.* Translated by Bernard Sahlins. Chicago: Ivan Dee, 1997.

———. *Entrées clownesques.* Paris: L'Arche, 1962.

Schechter, Joel. *Durov's Pig: Clowns, Politics and Theatre.* New York: TCG, 1985.

Scott, Diana. "Bang the Drum Slowly." *Callboard* (June 1993): 3–6.

Senelick, Laurence. *A Cavalcade of Clowns.* Santa Barbara: Bellerophon, 1992.

Towsen, John. *Clowns.* New York: Hawthorn, 1976.

Ward, Colin. *Anarchy in Action.* New York: Harper and Row, 1973.

Wiles, David. *Shakespeare's Clown.* Cambridge: Cambridge University Press, 1987.

Wilmeth, Don. *Variety Entertainment and Outdoor Amusements: A Reference Guide.* Westport: Greenwood, 1982.

Wilmeth, Don, and Edwin Martin. *Mud Show.* Albuquerque: University of New Mexico Press, 1988.

Lorenzo Pickle

An Interview with Larry Pisoni

L ARRY PISONI cofounded the Pickle Family Circus in 1974, planning the first circus season with Peggy Snider, Michael Nolan, and Cecil MacKinnon. Pisoni was a juggler and actor prior to becoming a clown and artistic director of the Pickle Family Circus. He learned juggling and other circus arts from Hovey Burgess and Judy Finelli in New York, where he also performed as a dancing gorilla at the Electric Circus and in Burgess's company, Circo dell'Arte.

Since leaving the Pickles in 1987, Pisoni has continued to perform clown acts with Circus Flora in St. Louis and in several one-person shows, notably *Clown Dreams*. He has taught clowning at the Ringling Brothers Clown College in Sarasota, at the Cornish College for the Arts in Seattle (where he served as artist in residence), and at San Francisco State University, where he directed his own adaptation of Henry Miller's clown story, *The Smile at the Foot of the Ladder*, in 1994, with Geoff Hoyle in the lead role. He has also directed stage plays for the San Francisco Mime Troupe and Teatro Vision (San Jose) and appeared in the film *Popeye*. His new show is called *Clown, Clown, Clown, Clown, Clown, Clown, Clown*.

This interview was conducted in San Francisco on August 31 and September 17, 1998.

Before you created the Pickle Family Circus, you were with the Pickle Family Jugglers and with the San Francisco Mime Troupe.

Yes, I taught circus techniques at the Mime Troupe, I was an actor, and I did Marxist-Leninist interpretations of children's puppet shows. I first saw the Mime Troupe perform *L'Amante Militaire* in New York the year that the Circo dell'Arte disbanded, at a time [when] I was involved in antiwar activities myself. Their *commedia* was very attractive to me; it helped me identify culturally with being Italian. I had been raised to be American, not Italian. My name originally was going to be Lorenzo, but it was given to me in American form as Lawrence.

When Circo ended in 1970, there was nothing keeping me in Manhattan. I decided to go to San Francisco, because the Mime Troupe could use someone who could do back handsprings and juggle. However, my goal was not to join the Mime Troupe; my goal was to put together my own alternative circus, after having taught the skills in various theatre companies. In my naïveté, I didn't call the Mime Troupe until I arrived in San Francisco; fortunately, Joan Holden [playwright at the Mime Troupe] was the one who answered the phone. I was there for three years. I also worked with a company called Gestalt Fool, the Firehouse Theatre, [and] a few other workshops.

After you joined the Mime Troupe, one of its political satires, Frozen Wages, *had most of the actors juggling Indian clubs in 1972. Were you an instigator behind the scenes for that play?*

It was largely Joan Holden and [Mime Troupe actor/director] Dan Chumley's scenario. I had been with the troupe for about a year, and one circus skill I was teaching to the collective, Indian club passing, was a good demonstration of group work, also a metaphor for group work. At that time we faced—we still face—the problem of the speed-up in production, on assembly lines, and elsewhere; and that was the problem *Frozen Wages* addressed. Juggling became a metaphor for speed-up technique. Before that play, we had been using pyramid building, stilt walking, acrobatics, and juggling as a come-on before the show. Dan Chumley and I also did a clown act as a preshow for a children's puppet show. We did a routine about standing on each other's shoulders, getting it done properly so he could make an announcement.

Impulses toward circus acts kept surfacing in your work with the Mime Troupe.

Before I moved to San Francisco, I performed with Hovey Burgess's group, Circo dell'Arte. Hovey, Judy Finelli, Cecil MacKinnon, and I combined *commedia lazzi* [comic business] with circus skills when we were together in New York. By the time I left Manhattan, I had already looked at a lot of circuses but hadn't seen one that I wanted to join.

What was it about existing circuses that displeased you?

Their aesthetic values, their social values, their business structure, their association (in the public's view) with carnival and the freak show. Now, with new circuses like the New Pickle Circus, there is a movement to inject story into circus. I think that the metaphors of each of the skills, each of the acts, are sufficient to the task of conveying a lesson. When you interject plot into a circus performance, it often slows the whole thing down because you need time for exposition and you need time to establish character.

What kind of circus did you want as an alternative to those when you started the Pickle Family Circus?

I looked at circus as a celebratory act: celebrating human experience and healthy relationships. This was long before people were used to talking about holistic systems. I was also concerned about the role of the performing arts group in the community, how it served the community, and how one defines community. My early Jesuit prep school education introduced me to some ideas about altruism and the giving of one's self for the betterment of the whole.

Dan Chumley once said to me, "You have great socialist instincts but no theory." I was very excited and inspired by the Mime Troupe's work on political issues, but I also remember sitting at Joan Holden and Dan Chumley's kitchen table in the early '70s and saying, "All I really want to do is make people laugh."

You didn't see yourself as a clown then? Did juggling lead you to clowning?

Yes, there is a connection. Hovey Burgess persuaded me that all circus skills are related; a juggler is an acrobat is a wire walker is a contortionist, and so on. Traditionally, if you are growing up in the circus and your uncle does a wire act and your aunt has a ball act, you're exposed to all the disciplines and acquire all the fundamentals. All the skills are related. So even when I was juggling, I didn't think of myself as a juggler. Juggling was the medium for my performance.

And when you were juggling, you wanted to make people laugh?

Yes, from the beginning, when I worked with Hovey and Judy, our juggling was done for comic effect. To achieve that comic effect, one has to have enormous technique. Hovey also taught us *commedia* for the Circo. And there was more to learn about comedy in the Mime Troupe. By the time I left the troupe in '73, Peggy and I had put together an act; we worked county fairs, college campuses, on the street. Then Cecil MacKinnon joined us. We created a comedy juggling act. My character was a Zampano [based on a character in Fellini's *La Strada*]—he thought he was in charge of the act, but in fact his partners were. I spoke with an Italian accent about how I was in charge, but ultimately the act demonstrated that the women were. Whatever politics I had at the time, I felt it was important to demonstrate them.

So your juggling act was about cooperation and who was in charge?

It was an act about how, if we worked together, we could create good stuff; but as soon as someone tried to be a star, the act would fall apart.

I think many of your subsequent clown acts showed that, too.

Yes, one of the aims of the Pickle Family Circus was to demonstrate that cooperative work could lead to the betterment not only of yourself but also [of] the community at large. Rather than try to teach that by talking about it, we would show it. One reason we were able to enjoy the support and enthusiasm of our audience when we gave a performance was that we would perform to help raise money for Bananas Daycare or for the Mission Childcare Consortium or the North Coast Senior Center. We went on fund-raising tours for nonprofit organizations which provided service to their community on a day-to-day basis, and that was the criterion for sponsorship. The traditional American circus business practice had been to enter a community and perform a benefit toward a group's annual picnic or Christmas tree fund. I wanted our circus to benefit child care in particular, at a time when women were becoming more active in the workplace and needed child care. We also tried to serve senior centers, food banks, environmental groups.

Did the Mime Troupe's collective form inspire some of the sharing of responsibility among the Pickle Family members?

Absolutely, although I made a distinction; I decided to call the Pickles a cooperative rather than a collective. This recognized that people who perform in the circus have individual skills—a wire walker would not necessarily be a great business manager. Then again, when our circus came to town, you could go out to the lot and see a bass player, a wire walker, and a clown all assembling the bleachers or all hanging canvas. We all worked together. Then, by the end of our performance, everyone was in the show, participating in *The Big Juggle.*

I saw *The Big Juggle* as a way to show people with many responsibilities and disciplines coming together. The closing image was that of a "feed," where everyone was throwing Indian clubs to one person who's the point of a triangle, and that person in turn was throwing the clubs back. There were circular formations, line formations, people throwing clubs over their shoulders, with multiple objects—six, seven, nine objects between two people—continuously forming geometric patterns. It was joyful, if not humorous, to see the guitar player leap off the bandstand to join in. The roustabouts also picked up clubs and came in, along with the clowns and Gypsy [Snider] and Lorenzo [Pisoni].

I've read several different accounts about the origins of the name of the circus. I'd like to think it's a sly, punning reference to a small ("piccolo" in Italian) family circus. But where did the "Pickle" in the title come from?

One time when Peggy, Cecil, and I were juggling in Central Park, an associate producer from a New York television show, *Wonderama,* saw us and said, "You guys are great. Would you be interested in coming on our Sunday morning show? We tape on Saturdays." We said, "Sure." Then she asked what we called ourselves, and my memory is, that was the first time I said we were the "Pickle Family." Earlier I had subscribed to a circus periodical, *Southern Sawdust,* under the name of the Pickle Brothers Circus; I don't know why I did that. But when we were asked for a name in the park, I looked at the three of us and said, "We're definitely not Pickle Brothers." In an instant, then and there, we agreed we were the Pickle Family Jugglers. That was how it began.

I spent a year raising money and finding people for our circus, and the pitch was that it would be the Pickle Family Circus. People would ask, "What's the Pickle Family Circus?" and I would answer, "It's Peggy, Sally [Cecil], Lorenzo (my performing name), and everyone else we can get together."

You once told me that it was a necessity for you to become a clown. What do you mean by that? You didn't seek out clowns.

I placed a want ad in the *[San Francisco] Chronicle* that said we were looking for jugglers, wire walkers, acrobats. I didn't list clowns; in the back of my mind I was thinking that I was going to clown. I had performed comedy with the Mime Troupe and *commedia* with Circo.

Among the people who auditioned for us was Bill Irwin, who had just finished eight weeks at the Ringling Brothers Clown College and decided it was not in his interest to join their circus. He had worked with Herb Blau, whose work I knew. He told me he danced, and one of my heroes was Ray Bolger. When Bill mentioned eccentric dancing, I knew what that was; the man with whom I first studied acrobatics had been an eccentric dancer. Bill also knew who Hovey Burgess and Carlo Mazzone-Clemente [founder of Dell'Arte in Blue Lake] were, and he had studied with the Japanese mime teacher Mamako.

So I invited Bill to our auditions at the Mime Troupe. He auditioned with a version of the spaghetti routine but without any spaghetti; it was a mime piece. I saw that this guy was exceptional; but I didn't want a mime in the circus, I wanted a clown. I told Bill that in the circus we have to see the spaghetti. He came up with the yarn business.

You were his partner when the act Spaghetti *opened the Pickle Circus in 1975.*

I was the chef, and he was the waiter. Basically, my job was to get Bill to go out of the kitchen and get us a customer. "We don't have any customers. How are we going to make a living if we don't have any customers?" I would ask. I was a mix of the Zampano character, my grandfather, and Chico Marx. I wore a chef's white hat and coat.

Years before in Euclid, Ohio, I had visited a famous vaudeville performer, Bobby May. He was a comedy juggler. He showed me some plate moves and gave me a set of juggling plates. Bill had the one plate move already. I gave him the plates that Bobby had given me, and Bill put together all his plate stuff, serving up the spaghetti and dropping it.

So Bill would go and get a customer in the audience, and then he would have trouble serving. The spaghetti stuck to the fork, fell on the floor, and so on; he ran out of spaghetti. What next? Ah, dessert, he gets a pie. I'm happy that the customer is finally going to get something. The audience thinks that the customer is going to get a pie in the face, but of course the waiter trips and it hits the chef (me) in the face. Chase, and that's the end. That's how I remember it, but there was an awful lot of improvisation. At one time, Geoff Hoyle, Bill, and I performed the act together; then we realized a third person wasn't needed. It was better with Geoff and Bill.

There was dialogue as well as physical comedy in Spaghetti. *I especially liked the comic reference to being a "wage slave." How did that come about?*

I think Geoff and Bill improvised the dialogue. The boss (the third man) became a character on the telephone. In the course of Geoff [chef] and Bill [waiter] trying to get dinner for their customer, the phone rings. Geoff: "It's the boss." Bill: "Ask him for a raise." And the boss says (via Geoff), "No more wages." Bill: "That's good; I no want to be a wage slave."

That's a line I'd expect to hear from Chico Marx after he performed with the Mime Troupe for a few seasons and then joined the Pickles. In your first season (1975), you also introduced a comic gorilla act.

We needed another act, besides the spaghetti routine, to fill out the first show. Bill had introduced me to Kimi Okada, his partner, who was a dancer.

My grandmother had been a dancer, too, in vaudeville; she tap-danced, and I learned to dance from her. In the Electric Circus in New York I had done a routine, a soft-shoe dance as a trained gorilla, with Judy Finelli, who tap-danced. As part of the act we kept upstaging each other. It ended with me—in the gorilla suit—hitting her in the face with a pie. So I had this idea for an animal act and proposed that Kimi and Bill would do this routine, in which she would be the tap-dancing gorilla, and it would end with the roles reversed; the gorilla would make Bill tap-dance.

Lorenzo Pickle, your clown, also danced with a number of gorillas in a later circus act choreographed by Kimi.

Lorenzo finds that after he's terrorized by these apes, the one way he can survive and thrive is to dance with them. Not only does he dance with them, but he's enjoying the dance. In the final image, he builds a pyramid with them, and he's the one holding all of them up.

You had another comic act about cooperation—or lack of it—in The Three Musicians. *Initially the trio of you, Bill, and Geoff looked quite dangerous, or at least driven, as the three of you entered in a line, staring straight ahead.*

The band was playing as we entered in step with one another, in a march, and then we struck a tableau of "Keep on Truckin'."

Did R. Crumb's cartoon (captioned "Keep on Truckin'") inspire the pose?

No, a vaudeville poster. The tableau was an extension of our step, with all of us leaning back at an extreme angle. We entered as close to one another as possible, striding in unison, making a big deal about extending the full leg, and breaking the line with a flexed foot, with big shoes on.

Bill Irwin, Larry Pisoni, and Geoff Hoyle *(from left)* in *The Three Musicians*. Photo by Terry Lorant.

While we're standing in tableau, the hat on each head comes off, it's twirled and goes straight up, then together we look out at the audience. We're there to play a song. Then the hats go back on our heads, we set the instruments down, and on the next cue, we all simultaneously do this hat manipulation. Invariably, one of us would drop his hat, and then we'd have to start the routine again and continue until we got it right. Then it was time to play music. The next step was to assemble our concert hall. It was like Goldilocks, with three chairs.

We all go to sit down. I'm wearing a fat suit, and I break my chair. Bill goes through the breakaway bottom of his chair. Geoff has the good chair. He comes around and helps me up from the ground. "I broke the chair, broke the chair," I'm crying. Meanwhile Bill's butt is stuck in his chair. Geoff and I attempt to extract him, in the course of which Bill gets his head stuck. He's doing a shoulder stand inside his chair. We ask, "What are you doing?" and he answers, "I'm practicing yogurt." So I'm behind Geoff, Geoff succeeds in pulling the chair off Bill's head, but he bumps into me, I fall down onto the ground, I do a foot pitch on Geoff's back, and he does a somersault over me (or was it Bill?). Then I get up and do a back handspring, falling into the arms of whoever is behind me.

Then the question becomes, who will sit in the last good chair? I sit, they both jump onto me, three of us are in the chair, and the chair falls over backwards. We all do somersaults, only I do mine holding onto the chair, and I end up sitting in it.

At last we play four bars of music, a tune written by Eric Leder. I play the trumpet, and my character, closest to rationality at this point, is responsible for getting the three of us together to play the tune. Geoff plays the trombone, after some trouble getting the slide to work properly. Bill goes off on a crazed drum solo. In the classic three-clown *entrée*, we end up playing a tune. The band joins us, there's applause, we take our hats off and do the hat routine again, and then we exit with the same march we used to enter.

Your clowning in that act and others approaches dance in some respects: it begins and ends with music and has a crazy, choreographed series of movements throughout.

Bill was a dancer, Geoff was a mime who obviously could dance, and I was really an acrobat. All three of those disciplines require repetition, muscle memory, flexibility, timing; in that sense, they are all related. Geoff admired music hall comedians; Bill had been doing mime and dance in Oberlin. It wasn't a big leap for us to have Kimi come in and choreograph work for us. I encouraged the band to write original music for the clowning, and we used a lot of sound effects, too.

Three Musicians was a routine about music, about the trio not playing it, or taking a long time to prepare to play it; but during the act, music was played by the Pickle Circus Band, not just by the three clowns.

Yes, the tune the band used to accompany us, not the tune we performed, was a variation on music that Chaplin wrote and sang as a waiter in his *City Lights.*

I knew there was something Chaplinesque about your comedy. I don't know if you would call the Pickle Family Circus "clown-centered," but I think at least during the first seasons, your three clowns made it distinctive and quite special.

When I was living in New York and had apprenticed myself to Hovey Burgess, if there was a circus within a hundred miles of New York, we went to see it. Not once did I see a clown act that I considered outstanding, with the exception of Otto Griebling [featured for many years in Ringling Bros. and Barnum & Bailey].

The problem I had with American circuses was that the clowns often were relegated to covering rigging changes. Their acts were prop-oriented and not character-generated. They weren't funny; they were just dumb, silly, or grotesque. Or their humor was based on the triumph of one individual at the expense of another, without redeeming social qualities. I was looking for something real in those clowns, and I didn't see it. On the other hand, I had seen films of European clowns, and I had been astonished by Buster Keaton. To me, Keaton was a great clown.

I felt that the role of the clown within the circus was quite important. So much of the circus has to do with the building up and release of tension, with risk taking and the triumph after taking the risks. The risk a clown takes comes from creating authentic and empathetic moments with his or her audience. You need to see yourself in me—the clown—and I need to project something that is truthful to you, that you see in yourself or someone close to you, and have that experience applicable to your life. It's a risk for a clown to show those qualities which are not so attractive to us and expose one's own sense of humor.

In the Pickle Family Circus I was so fortunate to have Bill and then later Geoff; here were two people who understood what it was to inspire laughter.

You once said that in the clown acts you were moving toward doing little plays.

Yes, I considered all of them to be that. They all had a little bit of a story to them; plot and character were essential. When I create a clown act, I start with an idea of where we want to be at the end of the routine. Bill, Geoff, and I would start with the simplest of outcomes; we would know how it was going to end. Over the course of working on the end, we would often find a better ending, but we had something we were working toward.

For example, when Geoff and I first performed *Sniff the Magnificent*, the premise was simple: Geoff was a bogus weight lifter, and Gristle, the character I played, was his manservant. At each and every opportunity, the manservant would unintentionally reveal the dodge by lifting the weights without effort or by lifting Geoff. (It ends with Gristle lifting Geoff as he— Sniff the Magnificent—holds the weights.)

You've also called that act "a Pozzo and Lucky routine." Was it influenced by Beckett's Waiting for Godot *characters in particular?*

I would say that all three of us (Bill, Geoff, and I) were and are still influenced by Beckett. We're all familiar with his work. Bill's Lucky [at Lincoln Center in New York] was phenomenal. And Geoff's production of *Endgame* in Berkeley was also quite wonderful.

I also had the good fortune to be directed toward Karl Valentin (the cabaret clown who influenced Brecht) by Ron Davis, the founder of the Mime Troupe. He invited me to a showing of Karl Valentin's films, and I was overwhelmed.

I consider myself a "new traditionalist" in clowning. I draw my inspiration from everything that has come before me. We build on each other's work. Any particular act is built on what someone else has done. Take someone like George Carl [an American clown who performed in circuses and nightclubs]. To some extent, the core of his club act has been around for a long time, and he developed it into something that was particular to him. But the whole business with the microphone cord, and shrinking inside of the jacket—Chaplin did it; it was being done in music hall and *commedia*. Students should go and see everybody's work, but not copy someone's act beat for beat; learn from what they did, and then make it your own.

Let me ask you how the character of Lorenzo Pickle developed. Did he exist before the Pickle Family Circus?

Originally, Lorenzo Pickle was one of the Pickle Family Jugglers. His character was loosely based on Anthony Quinn's character, Zampano, from *La Strada,* Chico Marx, and my grandfather, who was a vaudeville comic. To the extent that Lorenzo was like Zampano, he was patriarchal, he wanted to control everything, it was his show. He spoke with an Italian accent. As the chef in the spaghetti routine, he was the one who ran the place; the real boss never came around. We'd build Lorenzo up as the authority figure, and then he'd get the pie in the face. He definitely wasn't a whiteface; he was sort of a *contre-auguste,* middle-class, aspiring to authority but never up to the task.

When Geoff [Mr. Sniff] decided that he was leaving the circus and I decided not to do the juggling act anymore, Lorenzo changed. I began to do a red-nosed, baggy pants *auguste.* Around the country, there was all this talk: "Discover your inner child, blah, blah, blah." I thought to myself, here's an interesting opportunity. I can be a thirty-year-old ten-year-old who wants to try everything. (I had just turned thirty.) And because I was an acrobat, and I could walk a wire, and I played musical instruments, Lorenzo could jump up on a trampoline, do a back handspring, and could play with the band. So I was a ten-year-old in a thirty-year-old body. Ten-year-olds can be very serious; it was a way to explain Lorenzo's behavior—his enthusiasm for what he saw around him.

Did Lorenzo Pickle always carry a trunk?

I can tell you exactly where the trunk comes from. When I was seventeen and relocated to Manhattan, the only work I could get was in construction. I carried sacks of plaster dust and building materials. Another job I had was moving pianos.

Around the time that I made the metamorphosis from the Zampano Lorenzo Pickle to the red-nose Lorenzo Pickle, I genuinely felt the weight of the circus on my shoulders. So the trunk became a metaphor. Sisyphus pushes a rock; Lorenzo carries his trunk.

The Pickle Circus had so many acts with trunks in them. You, Bill, and Geoff all performed with trunks. Was this a conspiracy among the clowns?

Bill and Geoff worked together on a *lazzi* walking down the staircase in a trunk. It comes out of a classic mime act. Keaton did something like it in films. Bill and Geoff adapted it when they cut the back of the trunk out so that both of them could walk down and up "the stairs" in the same trunk. They would also fall into it.

In one act you carried Geoff inside a trunk on your back.

Yes. Any magician will tell you that one of the most difficult places to perform illusions is in a circus ring. So I thought, Geoff's not that big, the tuba doesn't weigh that much, I'll just carry them out in the trunk, and people will wonder how they got in there. The best magic tricks are done right in front of you; they are what they seem to be. It was much too difficult for me to pick the trunk up by myself with Geoff in it; so we would have four people pick up the trunk, and then I would crawl underneath it. I knew that if I could get it on my back, I could carry it.

It's quite a funny act, where you take the tuba out of the trunk and then turn away. We don't yet know Geoff is inside the trunk. How could it hold a tuba and a clown? Then Geoff gets out of the trunk and takes off his hat just as you had taken yours off.

Yes, and instead of balancing the tuba on his chin, as Lorenzo had, he takes the tuba and immediately turns it around and wears it as a hat. Sniff has his own logic; since it's too much work to balance the tuba, he'll just wear it as a hat. For him that's every bit as good as, if not better than, what Lorenzo did.

Eventually you both acquire tubas, Sniff sits on your shoulders, and you play a musical duet. It's a comic act, and part of it, like some of the others involving trunks, suggests there is endless space inside that box. It can hold two tubas and a clown; at other times clowns can walk down flights of stairs inside it, if they don't actually live inside it.

I never thought of the trunk as our residence. I could easily see Lorenzo Pickle as an itinerant on a dirty, dusty road somewhere, carrying his trunk.

If anything that he needs to do his act doesn't fit in the trunk, he's not going to use it.

Also, there's something magical about a locked trunk, out of which come musical instruments, hats, costume pieces, and juggling props. It's like finding an ancestor's belongings in storage in the basement, with old letters, photographs, clothing. For people who don't have anything to do with the arts or performance, the trunk also connotes time.

My grandfather's makeup kit was kept in a trunk in the basement. I have memories of going down there and opening up his old trunk and going through it. I remember at the age of seven finding spirit gum and coming up from the basement, with a mustache, to the chagrin of my grandmother. One of the first things you do with a small child is play peekaboo, and most children love it. It's similar when you open a trunk and then fall into it, disappear, then reappear.

The Multiple Sniffs *act had several trunks, with Sniff magically popping out of all of them, as I recall.*

It begins with my carrying in a trunk and setting it down stage left. Then I realize I only have one trunk, and I go off to get a second trunk. No sooner do I exit than the first trunk opens and Mr. Sniff pops out. He sees that I'm coming, closes the trunk, [and] exits without my seeing him as I come out carrying the second trunk, set it down, and realize there's a third trunk. I go off to get the last trunk, a much larger one. No sooner do I leave than Mr. Sniff comes out of the trunk which I just carried on.

The audience thought it was the same person?

He looked the same—exactly the same size as Geoff, in the Mr. Sniff wardrobe. I come back on again, carrying a huge trunk (with a false back). As I set it down, the second trunk lid opens up again, and Mr. Sniff gets out. He greets me and exits. Then while I'm looking in the second trunk, and my back is turned to the first trunk that I brought, the first trunk opens up [and] another Sniff gets out, closes the trunk, and exits before I see him. I run over to that trunk to see if there's somebody inside. Meanwhile, as my back is turned, another Sniff runs out and gets into the trunk that's behind me, and so on, leading to a chase with a little Sniff choreography by Kimi

Okada. There's an exchange between Geoff and me, then he takes my hat and starts running, only every time we run around the curtain, another Sniff appears, until I'm chasing seven of them. Geoff's there to taunt me with my little hat. I literally dive into a trunk and it closes; that's how it ends. In lots of ways it was about the trickster Mr. Sniff.

And those magical trunks, which hold an unlimited number of clowns. I think the image (opening that act and others) of Lorenzo carrying a trunk on his back is also compelling and universal—whether it's an artist or a tramp carrying his belongings.

In Bosnia, in the Congo right now, we see . . . refugees trudging with all their belongings—it's tragic and heroic at the same time. And in clowning, when you play pathos, you have to have room in the act so that it can turn around and be heroic.

Hugh Kenner titled one of the chapters in his Beckett book "Life in a Box." Was there a Beckettian "life in a box" implied by some of the circus clown acts with trunks?

In our circus we performed outdoors; our scenery was the sky, the stars at night. Certainly there was life in a box for those individuals fortunate enough to get carried in one. I for one was never carried; but my son spent a lot of time in a trunk as a kid. And poor Geoff Hoyle. We once gave a benefit performance, and we were going to do our act with two tubas. I was going to carry him on in the trunk. Two tubas were in there with him. I planned to open the trunk [and] have him stand on my shoulders and play the tuba; that was all we planned, three or four minutes at most.

So we walked in, ready to perform. I'm standing there with Geoff and tubas in the trunk on my back, and then the Stanford Marching Band decided it was time for them to perform. I held Geoff on my back for their first tune and thought they would go away. They played another tune, so I put the trunk down.

Without my knowing it (we had been rushing to get ready), Geoff had gotten into the trunk the wrong side up. Then it occurred to me, "Oh my God, he's on his head with these tubas!"

That's a comic act nobody saw.

You should have seen Sniff's expression when he got out of the trunk. It was an amazing moment. But we did play our tune, and then we got out of there.

By 1981, you, Bill, and Geoff had performed together outside the circus, first in Loose Ends *at Intersection for the Arts, then in* Three High *at Marines Memorial Theatre. Were you sensing a need to perform in other places, other forms?*

The three of us had seen some limitations to the outdoor show. We wanted more control of the environment. All of the clown material in the circus was written for a mixed audience (adults and children). I had a desire to write and perform material in a venue that was specifically for adults. In *Loose Ends* [produced by the Pickle Family Circus], we did clowning that we couldn't do in the circus, together and separately. There were some solos; Bill did one of the first versions of the harlequin that he does now, and Geoff was doing some violin stuff.

The basic premise for *Three High* was that each of us would write material that had roles for the other two. There were solo pieces, too. We had a live band. In *Three High* we also worked with Richard Seyd as our director; it was new for us to work with an outside director. (Of course, Kimi Okada had been there to choreograph for us.)

Eventually, in 1987 you left the Pickle Family Circus completely to do clown solos and other projects on your own.

After having been Papa Pickle (and artistic director) for all those years, having had the responsibility of the company both on and off the road, I needed not to do it anymore. Also, I had written a two-hour solo show, *Clown Dreams,* which was co-produced by the Pickle Family Circus and the Bathhouse Theatre in Seattle. Cecil MacKinnon, one of my juggling partners in the Pickles, became artistic director of Circus Flora and asked me to perform there. I've also worked with the Great Wallenda Circus and the L.A. Circus.

At Circus Flora I did a musical number with Cecil. She's a whiteface clown and ringmaster, and when I start playing the theme from *La Strada* on my tuba, she comes out and says, "Lorenzo, now's not the time to play." I take the tuba and balance it on my chin. She takes it off my chin and walks off with it. I pull out a pocket cornet and start to play the song, and she comes out again. I hear her coming, run over to a person in a box seat, and hand him the cornet. I tell her, "It was that guy." She comes over with an usher, and they take the guy backstage. I reach in the other pocket [and] pull out a silver fife to play the song from *La Strada*. She catches me, and I start to use the fife like a baton. Only this time Cecil produces a concertina. The two of us start playing, and the band joins us.

So your musical clowning goes on without the Pickles, with a new ringmaster!

It's been a great relief just to be a clown in a show, not the artistic director, and to go back to my trailer at the end of my act.

Willy the Clown

An Interview with Bill Irwin

BILL IRWIN performed as a clown in the Pickle Family Circus when it first opened in May 1975. As Willy the Clown, he was the partner of Larry Pisoni's Lorenzo Pickle in the first season, and late in 1975 they were joined by Geoff Hoyle, whose clown became known as Mr. Sniff. The trio of Irwin, Pisoni, and Hoyle developed several extremely popular clown acts, among them *Spaghetti, The Three Musicians,* and *Trunks.* In the first season, Irwin also performed a clown act with Kimi Okada, a dancer who became a choreographer for the circus in later years.

Prior to joining the Pickles, Irwin studied theatre, mime, and clowning. He was a member of Herbert Blau's Kraken theatre ensemble at Oberlin College and also studied mime with the Japanese artist Mamako. He completed the program in Ringling Bros. Clown College.

At the same time that he clowned for the Pickles, Irwin performed in other venues, notably at the Oberlin Dance Collective (ODC), which relocated to San Francisco after leaving Ohio. With Hoyle and Pisoni, he also toured San Francisco Bay Area schools. Their clown show called *Vinegar*

This interview was conducted on September 18, 1998, when Irwin was in San Francisco to perform *Fool Moon* with David Shiner at the American Conservatory Theatre.

was funded by CETA, and the three of them were CETA employees of the San Francisco Arts Commission for several years.

Irwin left the Pickle Family Circus in 1979, then returned in 1981 to perform during the winter season with Hoyle and Pisoni in a program titled *Three High,* directed by Richard Seyd at the Marines Memorial Theatre. The three clowns were reunited once again in 1985 for the *Pickle Clown Reunion* at San Francisco's Palace of Fine Arts.

Although Willy the Clown is rarely seen in a ring or onstage anymore, fragments and variations of clown acts developed with the circus could be seen in Irwin's later dance concerts and performance pieces, including *Not Quite, Still Not Quite, Largely New York, The Clown Bagatelles, The Regard of Flight,* and *Fool Moon.* Bill Irwin has also performed comic roles in plays by Molière, Shakespeare, Brecht, Fo, and Beckett and directed plays by Feydeau and Molière. He has appeared on television in *Northern Exposure, Saturday Night Live, The Tonight Show, The Cosby Show,* HBO's *Bette Midler: Mondo Beyondo,* PBS's *Great Performances 20th Anniversary Special, Third Rock from the Sun,* and *Sesame Street.* Films he has appeared in include *My Blue Heaven, Scenes from a Mall, Popeye, A New Life, Eight Men Out, Stepping Out, Hot Shots!, Silent Tongue, Illuminata, A Midsummer Night's Dream,* and *Ride with the Devil.*

How was Willy the Clown born? With spaghetti or without?

Here's the chronology I remember: In the 1974 student graduation performance at Clown College, another student named George Koury and I did a spaghetti serving act, which was a way for me to use a plate move I had learned. We didn't use any noodles, there was nothing on the plate; it was pantomime. I also had a shoulder roll I used to try not to spill a tray. We put together the four-minute act to use those moves.

It's fun to look back and see how something like that act came into being in order to use this little tumbling move, which was a very Chaplin-like move, incidentally.

At that time, my character was no "Willy the Clown" as such, but I did have his red wig and whiteface. There is a photo of him from the 1974 graduation—the Clown College pyramid of clowns.

At Clown College they gave us a pretty programmatic, fairly doctrinaire rundown of clown styles: "There's *auguste,* there's the whiteface, there's the carpet or tramp clown." *Auguste* clowning and carpet clowning styles interested me, but the look of the whiteface interested me, too.

At Clown College I tried different makeups. I took a white makeup of the sort that I had done mime with on the streets of San Francisco, added baggy clothes, and put the red nose and red wig on. It didn't really conform to any historical categories, but I liked the feel.

As to who Willy was, this is still an ongoing question. In the first season or two that I toured with the circus, my cousin, who had grown up with my family when she was young, said, "Willy reminds me a lot of your father."

One of my first memories of putting all this together was a publicity gig we did in San Francisco at a local school, before the circus had actually performed. We set up at Peggy and Larry's house on Potrero Hill and drove over to the school. They gave me a trombone, which I didn't know how to play and which came apart in my attempts. The kids all squealed when the red-haired clown came in, and as I recall, my main response was fear, being afraid in order to calm them. That was an early impulse in the character.

In the spaghetti act, when Willy wants to toss the plates, the chef keeps telling him, "Wipe, don't play." I'm wondering if that tendency to disobey and wander is part of his character.

Yes, very much, that was the case especially when Geoff and I were the duo, though always with fear of consequence.

What was it that drew you toward clowning?

I remember I had these notions of clowning as pure performance which haunted me. It pulled me away from the experimental theatre I was doing. I don't regret that theatre work—I treasure it; it still informs me, for better or worse, elitist or not. But I was pulled toward popular work. I would go to the Oberlin library and read books on clowns—such as they were—to get away from the academic, cerebral bent of the work of the theatre group I was a part of at the time.

In the first circus season, you did a comic tap-dance act with Kimi. You portrayed an animal trainer, and she was wearing a gorilla suit; by the end of the act, she had you dancing. Was that your first venture in eccentric dance?

I had always felt the impulse to dance. My study was tentative. I did a little at UCLA, a little at Cal Arts, a couple of modern dance classes. But I never could trust myself to remember a step. That gorilla tap-dance act was really the beginning of my learning to duplicate a step, which I'm still struggling with. Unless I really have to, I never do the same step twice, exactly the same.

In my mind, the trainer and the gorilla were going to be like Astaire and Rogers, or even better, Astaire and Eleanor Powell. I was no Astaire, but Kimi dancing in the gorilla suit made it a lot easier.

In the '70s, Kimi and I went to see *That's Entertainment* a couple of times and other films with dancing and comedy combined. In those days before the video was such a part of life, the only way to see films was to wait until they were shown at some theatre. Now, within minutes, I could be seeing any number of old musicals on video. I have shelves full of videos now. I often think: "Where was that when I was twenty-two and hungry for it?" You could also see the residue of vaudeville and music hall on TV in the '50s.

It was one thing to see eccentric dance on film and TV, but how did you learn to perform it?

Still working on it, as my legs wear out. The Pickles is where it had a place to blossom. When I came to the circus, I didn't have material. I came in response to an ad, and they asked, "What do you do?" I said, "Well, I just graduated from Clown College, I've done this, I've done that. . . ." "Do you have an act you can show?" they asked. "No, not really," I had to say. I saw Larry, Peggy, and Cecil's juggling act, and it was just mind-boggling to me. It was also source of anguish, turmoil, and envy. They would get a gig and ask what I was going to do. "I kind of . . . I don't know," I would say. I didn't have any material. After the circus began its shows, I would often just move as the Pickle band was playing. It was really an adjunct to their preshow numbers; it very gradually became something more. There exists a song which Phil Marsh of the original Pickle band wrote entitled "Hey Willy, Willy the Clown"—this was part of the come-in in early Pickle days, at the top of the show.

There's a choreographed entrance of sorts in The Three Musicians, *although most of the act shows the three of you out of sync, as you prepare to play music. You developed all of that comic movement with Geoff and Larry?*

Yes, like the blind leading the blind. The entrance was a kind of clown march, but none of us were choreographers.

Geoff Hoyle once said The Three Musicians *was created at a time when the three of you were "moving away from a heavy political style to a comic celebration of people triumphing over adversity." It was a comic act about trying to act together, or at least trying to play in concert, and it certainly didn't have a heavy political style. I don't think any of your acts did.*

In San Francisco, one of the important struggles for me was to come to terms with, to ingest and digest, the political ethos of the time, and especially the subculture, the San Francisco Mime Troupe. (The Pickle Family Circus can almost be seen in a way as an offshoot of the Mime Troupe.) At the time I was troubled by the social pressure and criticism in our subculture that things were not political enough. I was looking for a way to reflect a political outlook but at the same time trying to make fun of the self-serious "lefter than thou" attitude of our subculture.

Sometimes the Pickle Family Circus meetings would involve theoretical, political conversation, though mainly they were very practical. Other meetings among San Francisco artists were not unlike the '30s. Somebody would raise his hand and say: "I want to ask about Marxist-Leninist principles, and to what extent we adhere to them." And then the meeting would be over; to my mind, no practical work would then take place.

That joke about the boss and wage slaves in Spaghetti *does slyly make fun of political rhetoric.*

It's an old Marxist joke—Groucho's, I think.

Not the same Marxist principles the fellow at the meeting expected you to follow in the '70s. In those days, you didn't work in the circus all year round?

No, especially in the first couple of years, it was a very limited season. We often had nothing in between our weekend dates. Actually, that was great . . .

Compared to your current schedule of eight shows a week, you had a lot of rest between shows.

Yes, and it made no economic sense, but it was a wonderful time. In the 1978 season, rain wreaked havoc with our tour, and we looked back at the 1977 season and said, "*That* was why last year was so idyllic, because there was a drought." It was an awful year agriculturally, but it was a nice year to tour a circus.

For me it was a wonderful time of life. But it was not always easy. The CETA program came about because there was a recession. So there was always the question: "God, this profession! Is there really a living to be made?"

You moved around northern California with the circus tours for a few years; did all that travel inspire your clown acts with trunks? Or did the trunks come before the tours?

I used to show up for circus gigs with all this stuff in my arms and draped over my shoulder, and Larry said, "You need a trunk." I learned a lot from

Bill Irwin *(right)* and Geoff Hoyle share a trunk. Photo by Terry Lorant.

Larry and Peggy about logistics. The problem was that when I got a trunk, I used the trunk in the act—it created such a wonderful world—so I needed another trunk for storage, and so on.

Did you and Mr. Sniff have a name for your trunk act?

We just called it *Trunks.* It had pretty much the same setup as the harlequin act does now in *Fool Moon,* with the trunk against a drape. It was a very surreal act. Sniff and I never spoke to one another. I would stop and put a suitcase down, and Sniff popped out of the trunk and stole it. He would open the trunk when I wasn't looking and take everything into the trunk. Then we would run around the curtain, chasing each other. We were both inside the trunk for the curtain call.

When did you develop your special walk down three flights inside the trunk?

I remember I did half an evening with Doug Skinner in ODC's studio on Arkansas Street. It was in the mid-'70s. The trunk was just wedged into a corner of the room. I didn't know what to do at one point when I needed to make a costume change. I needed to go from having a hat on to wearing a conductor's wig. I was already in the trunk, so I just "went downstairs" to go out of sight—only one flight at that time. I hadn't gotten to the two tiers or three. A few people were there watching the rehearsal—Doug, Kimi, also Doug Winter the photographer, and Michael O'Connor, who was doing the other half of the evening. They laughed, and I thought, "There's something here!"

Later on I needed a name for what I had done at the Arkansas Street studio, because someone wanted to produce an evening of the work at the Margaret Jenkins Studio, and I said they were "not quite solo pieces," and the new show was called *Not Quite.*

And the sequel was called Still Not Quite.

Yes, followed by *Not Quite/New York* at the Dance Theatre Workshop.

After you developed the trunk act at ODC's studio, you and Geoff performed a variation on it in the Pickle Family Circus, descending several tiers. There's also an act where Geoff pushes you inside a trunk, although your leg hangs out of it, and Sniff prepares to saw off your leg.

Oh Lord, there were several different trunk acts. There was one against a backdrop, and another with freestanding trunks. Geoff and I revisited that act with the saw in 1990 at the Actor's Theatre of Louisville at a conference on *commedia dell'arte*. It grew out of the circus act, but we took it another step or two. In Louisville we did a thing where Sniff cut off my leg and carried it offstage. This left me some time in the trunk to give the illusion I had only one leg. You know one of Brecht's *lehrstück?*

The Baden Learning Play, *where the clowns saw limbs off a man named Smith.*

Yes, that may have been sort of culturally in mind, but it was mainly just the surreal gag notion: "Gee, he took it off, now I don't have a leg."

That immobility is very Beckettian, too.

Yes, it is. But *then* Geoff would reenter and do his three-legged dance. It was a great combination of material.

You know, Hugh Kenner has a chapter on Beckett titled "Life in a Box." Life in a trunk seems very Beckettian to me. You didn't have Beckett in mind when you developed the trunk acts?

No, or at least we were not consciously thinking about him. There are those figures in urns in Beckett's *Play,* and Nagg and Nell in the garbage cans in *Endgame.* Beckett and *Sesame Street* cross with Oscar in his garbage can. Who knows where images really spring from? Maybe it's just that as soon as you get a trunk, it makes a great prop and a world to inhabit.

The image of a clown in an old tuxedo carrying a trunk, or living in one, is quite evocative. Was your trunk act reflective of a tramp's life, or more of a surreal image?

More the latter. The story existed only there in the performance. I remember being asked, "Does Willy live in the trunk?," and in a radio interview, for instance, it was interesting to say, "Yes, he has a trunk instead of a trailer." But in fact, the idea of inventing a life for him didn't interest me as much as the space of time onstage.

It's just an act in the ring, in a trunk, the way the spaghetti act is first of all juggling plates. The performance aspects of the act come to the fore.

I guess so. I remember one review of *Largely New York* striking a chord when it talked about how the action "exists only in the theatre."

You know that famous statement by Beckett about Joyce? He refers to Finnegan's Wake *and says it is "not about something; it is the thing itself." Beckett also offers actors a chance to perform in the immediate situation, on a bare stage. I feel there was something like that in the Pickle clown acts as well.*

Yes, there was. Partly just by necessity. And when you say "bare stage," that recalls an ongoing joke between me and Nancy Harrington [producing stage manager of *Fool Moon*]. She likes simplicity. Whenever we talk about elaborate props, she says, "I like the actor and the bare stage," and she's most often right.

I remember years ago, Herb Blau told us with some pride about his production of *Waiting for Godot* here in San Francisco. *Waiting for Godot* is a play I love and want to do again and again; but at the time he was telling us this, I didn't get that play at all. At one point, when Gogo says, "I'm hungry," Herb said he had the actor pound the edge of the proscenium, as if to say, "I'm hungry and I want to break this proscenium." The irony is that the bureaucratic response to the hunger Herb was talking about in the '60s and '70s was to build those god-awful theatre facilities that we're all stuck with now. Black boxes and cut-rate thrust stages. I remember Herb talked about this actor striking the proscenium with passion and pride; it was like hearing somebody talk about their marching in the big general strikes of the '30s, or fighting in the Spanish Civil War, and hard for us to fathom because there were so few proscenium stages left, for a while.

If the actor had broken the proscenium, it would have been Beckett with even less than a bare stage. But that kind of acting is not just on a bare stage, the stage is practically another character; it's acting with the building, with the theatre.

Yes, and with the audience.

Which you would have to do in the circus, too.

Exactly. But in many ways, it's a radical notion in institutional theatre. That's what *Fool Moon* does in a way; it brings a bit of circus ethic into the ornate, classical frame of the proscenium.

As if circus clowns have taken over the theatre?

I should clarify my perception there. I am somebody who worked in the theatre, then got interested in the circus, and now have returned to the theatre. And in fact, my credentials in circus are kind of limited. David Shiner, my partner in *Fool Moon,* has done much more circus work and more street work than I have. Whenever I go to the Ringling show or go to teach at the Ringling Clown College, I have to be careful; it would almost amount to affectation or pretense to talk too much about my circus experience. David talks at times about missing the circus, by which he means European-style shows. I have a more diffused connection. I have a nostalgia for that time with the Pickle Family, but I don't really miss the camping out, the truck driving, and the bleacher setup. It's not a country for old men.

You were never simply performing for the circus; you were creating other events, too?

Yes. Benefits, community shows, lots of things. Because Larry, Geoff, and I were CETA artists, we did a lot of work outside the Pickle Family Circus, in the city schools. We had these shows we called *Vinegar*. It was actually a fair amount of the work we did together, because the circus had a limited season. We cannibalized our circus acts. This was arranged through the San Francisco Arts Commission, and it didn't cost the schools anything. The schools were desperate for performance events.

So we did a lot of 8 A.M. shows. I made up as Willy, Geoff as some early version of Sniff, Larry as Lorenzo Pickle. I remember standing behind a curtain, waiting for the cue to go on, as I still do today in *Fool Moon*. We would put our shoes under the curtain: one big shoe, two big shoes, six big shoes. Squeals of laughter from the kids. Then we would do *The Three Musicians,* usually a twenty- or thirty-minute show. I remember taking questions afterwards. We must have done two or three dozen of those.

That would have given the three of you more time to collaborate.

Yes. If you look at the Pickle Family Circus calendar, there weren't all that many shows in the '70s. We worked together much more in things like *Vinegar.* And it was pure clowning.

Clowning is an ephemeral art; like acting, it vanishes after the performance, in most respects. And yet it lives on. Parts of the old Pickle acts live on in your current performances and in Geoff's and Larry's.

It is not only still alive, but for something so ephemeral, you would think it would bear very little resemblance to what somebody was doing 30, 40, 150 years ago, but books suggest that there's a great resemblance. Look at

Cirque du Soleil, where Geoff and David have performed and [where] Larry and Peggy's children, Lorenzo Pisoni and Gypsy, now perform. Circus skill acts may have changed to a great extent, but I think clowning has not. There is actually a continuity, or at least a continuation.

Mr. Sniff

An Interview with Geoff Hoyle

G EOFF HOYLE joined the Pickle Family Circus for the fall 1975 season and performed as a clown through 1981. He returned to perform in the 1984 winter show at the San Francisco's Palace of Fine Arts and in the *Pickle Clown Reunion* in 1985. He created several characters in the circus, most notably sausage-nosed Mr. Sniff, and partnered with Bill Irwin and Larry Pisoni. After leaving the Pickles, he performed as a guest clown at several other circuses, including Cirque du Soleil and Circus Flora. He has acted in plays at many prestigious American theatres, including the Eureka Theatre, the Berkeley Repertory Theatre, the American Conservatory Theatre, the American Repertory Theatre, La Jolla Playhouse, and Northlight Theatre. Hoyle was cast in lead roles in plays by Fo, Brecht, Beckett, Jonson, O'Casey, and Shakespeare. With director Tony Taccone, he developed and toured the solo shows *Boomer!, The Convict's Return, Geni(us),* and *The First Hundred Years.* For more than a year he was in the original Broadway cast of the *The Lion King,* directed by Julie Taymor.

This interview was conducted in San Francisco on November 11, 1998.

It's hard to believe Mr. Sniff is not as old as the Pickle Family Circus; he was part of it for so many seasons. But you created other clown characters first.

One routine I did for the Pickles in the fall of 1975 involved "the guy in the audience," Harry Kershaw. (I joined in the end of the first season.) Harry was the shill, somewhat disguised as an audience member. His costume was a bright red plaid suit, a tie in the same plaid, and a bowler hat. He was annoyingly eager and eventually muscled in on an act. Larry Pisoni had an incredible routine, where as Lorenzo Pickle he would carry a tray of glasses across the ring, up some steps, then down, add another tray on top of the first, walk back, until he was balancing ten or fifteen trays of glasses. Harry Kershaw was the guy who made him drop the glasses when he tried to help.

When Lorenzo Pickle got mad, Harry said, "I just wanted to help and be in the show, I love it so much." So Lorenzo asked, "What can you do?"

When I offered to play my violin, Lorenzo said, "This is a circus; you can't just play the violin." He had me play the violin on a rolla bolla. It would have been more impressive if I had been able to play the ocarina while balancing on my hands on the rolla bolla. That was the first circus act I ever did.

The next act I did was *The Three Musicians,* with Larry and Bill, the following season. It was a classic clown routine, based on a trio like the famous Fratellini brothers. In our case, the silent heavy was played by Larry in a fat suit. My character's name was Bushybeard, because I had a beard at the time, and I was a put-upon but irascible thin guy. Bill was the *contre-auguste,* like Albert [Fratellini], completely incompetent, unable to do anything, but extremely anxious.

We entered with a little dance, which finished with a few hat moves. Larry had a tuba case. I had a trombone case. Bill entered with a bass drum with a cymbal attached to it. We would put these things down and go into our hat moves, sometimes messing them up. It was all done with Italian accents. "Now we got to play the music. But first we need a the chairs." There was a series of disasters with the chairs.

There were three chairs preset onstage. One had the bottom fall out after I sat in it, and I couldn't get out. I would run around on all fours on the floor with my butt in the chair. Bill managed to get me out of there; I took a fall. Simultaneously, Bill took a dive and got his head stuck in my chair, upside down. Then I pushed Bill's head out with my foot, causing him to catapult backwards, knock Larry down, and do a back flip over his feet, followed by a double Eskimo roll. Meanwhile, I now had my foot caught in the chair . . . you get the idea. Bill and I did a bit where he takes a chair and sits on it, and I pull it away to sit on it, then he takes it away. Eventually we weren't even pulling away the chair. We were just getting up, turning around, and falling down. That second chair was demolished, too.

Then we looked at the third chair, which had never moved. Pisoni, the fat guy, sat on it, and it collapsed completely. The back was rigged to fall from the front. (We had replaced all the screws with matchsticks before the show.) So we didn't have anywhere to sit, except the chair whose bottom had fallen out. All of us did a backward roll. Pisoni did his holding the chair. Somehow we ended up with Pisoni sitting on that chair and Bill and I sitting on his thighs. Then standing. We finally all sat down, which made us all very happy. The point had been to sit down and play music; it was that simple.

Then we got up and opened the instrument cases. Out of the tuba case Pisoni would pull a pocket cornet. I would pull a trombone out of my case, and Bill would tune up the drum and cymbal. I would have trouble putting my trombone together. Then there were several false starts followed by Larry counting off, "One, two, three," and we played the tune. After the tune, we did a couple more hat moves, then did our choreographed walk off in unison.

Everybody loved *The Three Musicians.* We brought it back several times later in benefits. I believe we could put it together again if we had to.

The three of you created that act together, by improvising in rehearsals?

Yes, that was the great thing about our trio; we all brought our various disciplines to it. Larry had been raised as an acrobat by an uncle who taught him acrobatic tricks. The closest I got to that was to throw a back handspring. Bill had his full dive into a hat, which he still does. Of course Bill also had his clown character, his mimetic training, and his eccentric dance training. I had my mime training, and my irascible, satirical approach to performance—a very English music hall kind of character. And Larry had developed his Italian Lorenzo Pickle.

A lot of the act was improvised. First we decided on the hat moves. Then, "We need an entrance," so we worked on an entrance. We did a march. Someone would say, "I got a move, then we could do the hat thing." We got about fourteen things in a row and would end up with three. Knowing how to cut is half the battle.

Looking back, do you see a subtext or special theme behind the act? Larry Pisoni suggested that some of the acts were about cooperation, or lack of it.

When we were asked to philosophize about the circus, and what made it different, one of the answers would revolve around statements like, "The clowning isn't mean-spirited, it's not demeaning, the violence is accidental." We would say the clown acts were about cooperative work, about joy-

Geoff Hoyle as the chef and Bill Irwin as the waiter (with broken ankle in cast) perform *Spaghetti*. Photo by Terry Lorant.

ful sharing in attempting an insurmountable task, though sometimes I think we just said that for the benefit of the grant givers. In fact, we wanted to be as anarchic and outrageous as we could.

The routines were also about the injustice of the class structure or bureaucracy, though we weren't the San Francisco Mime Troupe; we never tried to be that. But there were implications. Take the *Spaghetti* routine. To create a dramatic propulsion for that scene, we created an offstage presence, Il Padrone, The Boss, at the other end of the phone. The clowns were underdogs, "I'm a working guy," working people in conflict with some authority, which would engage the audience's sympathy on the side of the put-upon little guy.

In The Three Musicians, *the three clowns are in conflict with one another.*

They're in conflict with the damn chairs. They battle the tyranny of things. The chairs won't cooperate. They're also in the extremely exposed and pressurized situation of having to perform. That was the real setting: "We're here, we're three musicians, we're going to play. You're there, the audience, and we're going to play to *you.* Whoops."

It's a comedy about having to perform.

Yes. It was about performance. The antagonist is the performance situation itself.

You have that in the Spaghetti *routine, too; the restaurant workers have to perform for the boss and the customers (in the audience)—serving dinner is an art, too.*

Yes. We set up an audience member as the client [and] gave him a huge knife and fork and bib, which was for many years one of Bill's white shirts with the sleeves tied together. Whenever Bill went out to the audience as the waiter, he would smooth his hair, to look suave and smooth. But what goes on "backstage" in the kitchen is horror. "This is the last spaghetti." "What are we going to do?" "You just got to relax." "I don't know if I can do this." So we had to perform and do something we were not up to.

I don't think the same questions can be asked about your trunk acts. Stepping inside a trunk, or being carried inside one, did not confer high status on your character. You were more like luggage.

Sometimes we called those acts our "clown haiku," because they were little, self-contained, wordless metaphors of antagonistic relationships that had a resolution to them. They were distillates of clown archetypes. You could say we used clown archetypal props: musical instruments, chairs, and trunks. Trunks come out of the history of nomadic performance, where what you had is what you carried in your trunk—your bag of tricks and your personal belongings were transported in them on the vaudeville circuit, or with the circus.

But you transported people in those trunks?

In the ring, everything is possible; yes, you can put people in trunks. And people can pop out of them. It's a metaphor. In *Multiple Sniffs,* Larry as Lorenzo brings on the trunk, opens it up, I pop out as Sniff, and then go back in. He brings out another trunk, and I pop out again. He can't figure out how I'm in two different trunks. This happens five times. We had five Sniffs. I'm running circles around him. It literally becomes a chase, with him trying to catch one, two, many Sniffs.

Sniff is irrepressible; they can't keep him in a box.

That, or it's just a nightmare. *Trunks* started out with Bill, Willy the Clown, as a traveler bringing out his luggage. Willy is going somewhere with suitcases, trunk, a set of golf clubs, a ski pole mixed in. He puts down the luggage [and] goes off to get something he forgot. Mr. Sniff comes out wearing a customs officer's hat; he represents authority, organization, repression. Or what Willy might consider to be authority, repression, and organization. In fact, Sniff has his own anarchic sense or "non-sense" about him.

Sniff is an annoying authority figure; he's like a mosquito. At one point the trunk opens. Sniff pressures Willy into giving up his cane and hat, takes out a card and stamps it, and gives it to Willy as a kind of coat check. He descends into the trunk as if it were his office. He pulls out a saw, and we hear a sawing sound. But he closes the trunk—his office is closed. Willy, bewildered, raps on the trunk and gestures for his hat and cane. Sniff gestures, "Your claim check." He takes the check, descends into the trunk, and gives Willy his hat and then his cane, now only six inches long. "Thank you," gestures Willy. With a suspicious eye on Sniff, he takes the cane to lean on it without looking and takes a huge fall, head first onto the ring cloth. Sniff thinks this is all perfectly normal. It's what you get when you don't pay attention.

When Willy gets up, Sniff is poker-faced. Willy asks: "Did you . . . cut that off?" Sniff says definitively, "ME? . . . Cut that off?" He says accusingly, "Yeah . . ." And Sniff says, "Yeah . . . ," which completely flummoxes Willy. The children in the audience had been shouting, "It's him, he did it!" But that shut them up. I think it floored them that anyone would admit their misdeeds. The adults, of course, roared with delight.

The act continued. Willy turns the trunk around, and Sniff sits on the edge, suspiciously. Willy would start telling him jokes. He'd push Sniff off the trunk, and Sniff would bounce back twice. The third time, Sniff is annoyed; he brings out a handkerchief, cleans off the trunk, and gestures to Willy, "Why don't you have a seat?" When he is about to sit down, Sniff flips the trunk open, Willy falls in, and the trunk slams shut, except one of Willy's feet is sticking out. Sniff starts to saw off the foot.

But Willy's hand comes out, in a white glove, and shakes a reprimand at you for even thinking about that.

But I did saw the foot years later, when we did Bill's play about pantomime clown George Fox in Seattle. Then I would take the false leg off stage and come back as the three-legged man, do a little dance, and go out. We did that in Seattle and Louisville.

Your dance as the three-legged man is a wonderful, classic act. Did you create that while you were with the Pickles?

I developed that for a Pickle Family benefit in the early '80s. I performed it (as Sniff) in Circus Flora and in Cirque du Soleil. Had I developed it earlier, I might have done it in the Pickle Family Circus, too.

You did some other dances in the ring. Remember "The Boing Boing Boogie Woogie"?

That was a preshow warmup. Phil Marsh wrote the words. "The Boing Boing Boogie Woogie Bounce" was introduced as a participatory tune, for the audience to sing along, although Mr. Sniff didn't say anything. The chorus went "Boing Boing, Boing Boing Boing Boogie Woogie. It's the

Boing Boing Boogie, the Boing Boing Boogie Woogie Bounce." I carried stop sign–shaped paddles. On one side it said "Boing and Boogie," on the other side, "Woogie and Bounce": I was the bouncing ball, and I did this crazy bouncing dance, cuing the audience to sing the words on whichever paddle I held up.

At a certain point in the dance, Sniff would get tired, at least in the Alaskan television version I saw recently. Sniff starts off energetic, constantly bouncing, and gets worn out.

I don't remember that, but it makes sense. Sniff is constantly revealing the soft white underbelly, as it were, behind the bravura, the "magic" behind the trick, as if to say: "Hey, we're really circus performers, and we're really tired, and you have no idea how hard this is." But Bill was the dancer [among us]; he was the one who would break into the tap stuff. Occasionally I would parody him. Then later, after I left, they had the multiple gorilla dance, choreographed by Kimi.

While it wasn't exactly a musical or dance act, one trunk routine had Sniff proudly wearing a tuba on his head like a hat, with the bell covering everything down to his neck. How did that scene come about?

That was the act which began with Sniff inside a trunk with a tuba. Lorenzo carried it on. Lorenzo balanced a tuba on his chin, and Sniff thinks, "Piece of cake," and puts the tuba on his head bell down, pretending to balance it. "Ta da!" Sniff thinks this is an equally good trick.

Mr. Sniff also sometimes parodied other circus acts. "Sniff the Magnificent" was a bogus weight lifter. He was also "The Human Bomb," a human cannonball.

Yes, at the Palace of Fine Arts we made this big cannon. Larry played Gristle, my downtrodden assistant. I got into the cannon and was fired off with Gristle's help. Moments later, my feet could be seen sticking out of the back wall of the house as if I'd gone through the wall headfirst.

You flew over the audience, from the stage to the back wall, in a blinding flash?

Yes, we had set up a tiny net to be held by audience members halfway down the house so they could catch me. Then the audience would hear a boom, a whistle. A spotlight would focus on the net, then find me at the back of the house. Sniff's feet would be sticking out of the wall, then he'd lever himself back out, completely blackened face, all of his clothing completely ragged. He'd stagger back to the stage, embracing the women and children and shaking hands with the men. He'd then drink some champagne. To this day Bernie Weiner, former theatre critic for the *Chronicle*, asks me how I did it.

How did you first create Mr. Sniff's character (if you can reveal that)?

He grew out of the irascible nature of Harry Kershaw, the audience shill. Larry, Peggy, and I were trying to figure out a character that I could do in the show after *The Three Musicians*. I'm not sure whether Larry or I thought of a big nose. Larry and Peggy came up with the idea of a long coat. We looked at old clown illustrations as part of our research. For instance, there's a wonderful book, Disher's *Clowns and Pantomimes*. One of the clowns pictured was a sinister-looking guy with a big hat, dark glasses, and a long coat. That looked interesting, so I did some drawings of a clown with a big nose, bowler hat, and a long coat. Larry said, "It's Mr. Sniff." Larry wanted to make the coat yellow because it was a circus color. I probably would have chosen a dirty mac, which would have been more of a theatrical choice. But a yellow coat was very much in the style of the Pickles, who had vibrant primary colors. I had the bowler hat from *The Three Musicians* and had been practicing hat moves, which Bill, Larry, and I would share with each other and try to create a vocabulary.

As for the nose, it's very pragmatic; but at the same time it comes out of one's particular temperament. I think I went down to the makeup supply store and said, "Give me a bunch of noses." I knew I couldn't use a Willy nose; he had a red bulbous one. I found this big long thing, which was absurd. How could one possibly wear it? It looked like a *commedia* nose, with some aspects of Pulcinella, though his is much more hooked. Sniff's nose has an obscene factor to it: a long phallic nose, red at the end. Because it was such a big nose, it became clear that Sniff would investigate most things by smelling them. And since I *have* an acute sense of smell, it all fell into place. Sniff the clown, like all clowns, is really a projection of aspects of the performer's personality.

We created a battery of different sound effects for Sniff's nose. Keith

Terry came up with the best one; he would rub an oatmeal box top in front of a microphone for the sniffing sound. Cirque du Soleil subsequently tried to duplicate that sound by sampling it on a synthesizer and pressing a key when Sniff performed for them. Therein lies the difference between the Pickle Family Circus and Cirque du Soleil: from oatmeal box to electronic synthesizer. And the synthesizer never worked. You need a live person to time it and be keyed in for those effects.

You were much more in tune with one another, so the band would know when your character needed the oatmeal box sound effect. After an ensemble has worked together for a year or two, they know one another.

Yes, I did seven seasons with the circus, and they got to know Sniff well. There was a different working relationship. It wasn't compartmentalized, and it wasn't only virtuosic or star-driven. We were working as an ensemble, collectively producing and managing the work. When we did our theatre show, *Three High,* AGVA [American Guild of Variety Actors] tried to unionize us. But they didn't know what to do with us. There was no management to negotiate with.

Since you left the Pickles, you've acted in many plays, in experimental and regional theatres, and on Broadway. Do you see yourself as an actor, not a clown, in the plays?

I see acting and clowning as parts of the same continuum, maybe extremes with circus clowning at one end and Chekhovian acting at the other. When I'm acting I'm not necessarily clowning; but when I'm clowning, I'm always acting. In the clown acts we used all of our acting skills. The makeup, costume, and movement were quite grotesque, but the acts were always nailed to a detailed portrayal of realistic characters reacting in real situations.

I think my clown work contains some of the best acting I've done; and the acting work contains some of my best clowning. There was a big difference from the circus in the use of speech for Fo's play, *Accidental Death of an Anarchist.* Although we did some verbal clowning in the Pickles, early on we decided that in the open air, with an audience that was constantly in movement and had a multigenerational spread, many verbal gags were not going to work. We had a hard time being heard outdoors in the ring, although we found ways to be heard there, by making the speeches short and making them repeat key ideas.

When I did *Accidental Death*, I felt that I was proving to the theatre community that I could work in a play, that I could not "just be a clown." Before I did Fo's play there, the Eureka Theatre was doing lots of incredible work, and I was not involved in any of it. The Pickle Family Circus was a parallel universe, respected and approved of as part of a progressive, popular, nontraditional, experimental cultural movement that happened in the late '70s and early '80s. But it was parallel; we didn't cross over. I was sad that I was not able to be in the play *Comedians* at the Eureka. I felt: "Oh, they think I'm just a clown."

Now when I "routine" in a solo show, and it's not verbal, perhaps more than other times my acting is informed by my work with the Pickles and by my research into clowns and silent film comedians. This was the case when I did "The Conductor," and the scenes with Doris the python and the chair in *The Convict's Return;* "Hoylo the Conjurer" and "The Dance of Death" in *Geni(us);* Antoine's violin act and the *auguste's* routine with the moon in *The Smile at the Foot of the Ladder;* the routines with crockery and bottles in my new show.

You had some experiences with what's been called "New Circus," such as Cirque du Soleil shows in which acts are integrated in a story.

The most recent Cirque du Soleil shows' narratives are so vague and abstract, they become to my mind almost pretentious. "It is about everything, because it is about nothing." I would agree with Mr. Sniff: "If it's about nothing, it's about nothing."

Was Cirque du Soleil different when you performed with it in Nouvelle Experience?

I think it was the same, but perhaps the acts had slightly more thematic and narrative linkage. It was about an Everyman figure plucked from the audience and thrown into a fantastic universe where he goes through a series of encounters with devils and strange comic figures who speak nonsense. I feel that hides a multitude of sins; it's as if they don't want *ideas* to distract you from their lovely, fantastical, whimsical costumes, decor, and lights.

And merchandizing. It's the triumph of form over content. It can result in a dreadfully bland though admittedly eye-catching kind of corporate-sponsored art, which doesn't engage the audience emotionally or intellectually.

You also see it in shows like *The Lion King;* do the characters and story have to be so vastly oversimplified and the message so politically reactionary? For example, after his father takes him up Pride Rock and shows him the kingdom, Simba asks, "You mean all this will be mine?" The implication is yes and that's good. It's an interesting message . . . one which promotes the value of power and hereditary wealth rather than, say, wisdom and compassion. And then, unlike in a traditional folk or fairy tale where the hero has to go through fire and ice to become king, Simba doesn't really have to learn or do anything. But hey, it's only a Disney story, right?

My new show, *The First Hundred Years,* is about a clown holed up in a theatre which is being demolished to make way for a corporate retail, sports, and "disastertainment" center. The demolition of the theatre in the show is a metaphor for the destruction of the traditions of live entertainment which are being dumped in favor of managed fun and electronic entertainment. In clown terms, easy laughs. The show tries to address questions about the uses of art and the function of comedy, also about how we utilize public space, about urban planning and which decisions inhibit or promote civic discourse. Are we in danger of giving away control in these areas to global megacorporations? I wonder, do they really have the best interest of an informed citizenry at heart? But I'm just a curmudgeonly old clown. At the end, he dodges the wrecking ball. He's a survivor. Like an old gunfighter, he straps on his guns one last time . . .

Doesn't clowning transform that discontent into comedy and satire? I've seen that happen in your performances.

Hopefully the clown transcends discontent by celebrating the human spirit. My favorite photo of all time for that aspect of clowning was the one of Dario Fo in the old Eureka Theatre greenroom. He has arms outstretched in a shrug with a wide toothy grin, which seems to be asking ironically: "Doesn't it all make complete sense, eh?"

4

Spaghetti
A Clown Act by Larry Pisoni, Bill Irwin, and Geoff Hoyle

T HE SCENE *begins with the chef [Lorenzo when Pisoni played it, Tony when Hoyle played it] and waiter [Irwin's Willy the Clown] high-stepping into the ring, one behind the other, Willy in front, with musical accompaniment. Willy wears a formal long black jacket, black trousers, black bow tie, bright red wig, whiteface, and bulbous red nose. The chef wears a large, floppy white hat, white coat, and white pants.*

Willy takes off his jacket; Tony offers him another. Willy tries to put it on, but first puts the back of the coat and its arms in front of him.

Tony: Subito. Lavorare, lavorare, Willy, worky, worky, worky.
Willy: I can't a get this . . . I can't a . . .

This reconstruction does not fully convey the physical comedy and musical accompaniment performed during the act. Some of the dialogue and action in the scene can be seen in the film *Putting Up the Pickles.* However, the act changed with improvisation during the years it was performed. There is no definitive version.

(Tony helps him. They count to three together during their effort, and with difficulty Willy spins and the coat falls into place. Willy takes a white plate, wipes it with cloth, and starts to flip it.)

Tony: Willie, wipe, don't play.

(Willy flips the plate quite high, catches it with hand, then tosses it with foot, catches it, smiles at successful toss. Drum roll accompanies the plate's flight.)

Tony: Willy, wipe. What will Il Padrone . . .
Tony and Willy (in unison, with fear): . . . The Boss!
Tony: . . . have to say about this? You could break the plate . . .

(Tony bends toward the floor, as if to catch falling plate, and hurts his back.)

Willy: Have you break a the back? I'm a give you chiropractic.

(Willy lifts Tony up, twirls him around, in variation of jitterbug twists, accompanied by music.)

Willy (hears phone): The telephone.
Tony: It could be Il Padrone . . . the Boss.

(Alarmed, Tony jumps into Willy's arms. Willy holds him like a bride in groom's arms before threshold.)

Tony: Answer him.
Willy: Okay.

(He drops Tony, who falls on ring cloth.)

Willy: Tony, I'm a hope that is the Boss. We can tell him that we're a
    tired to be . . .

(They strike heroic poses.)

Together: . . . a wage slave!
Willy (takes the old-fashioned two-piece phone): Hallo, si . . .
(He covers the earpiece but not the mouthpiece.) Tony, it's a the Boss. Yeah,
  it's old Fatso he-self.

*(Tony points and Willy, too late, switches so as to cover the mouthpiece. They
exchange fearful looks and do little dance steps of discomfort as Tony speaks.)*

Tony: Hallo, si. Si Signor, si. Spaghetti, rigatoni, macaroni, ravioli . . .
  si, Signor.

(He hangs up.)

Willy: Tony, I hope you told the Boss that I'm a tired to be a wage slave.
Tony: Si, Willy, si.
Willy: What he say?
Tony: No more wages.
Willy: What?
Tony: Now we worken on a commission.
Willy: What a means commission?
Tony: No customers, no pay.
Willy: Tony, we got to find . . .
Together: . . . a customer!

*(Willy takes giant red menu, goes into audience in search of a customer. Ties
one very large white bib around audience member or around the necks of two small
children seated next to each other. Gives them giant eating utensils, then walks
back to Tony.)*

Tony: How much he get to eat?
Willy and Tony (look at customer together and speak with enthusiasm): He's
  a big one.

[In some versions, "1," "2," or "3" was printed on the menu, and there was interaction with the audience.]

(Tony reaches into large metal pot with fork and tosses a ball of spaghetti— white and stringy—to Willy, who tries to catch it on the plate. This is repeated several times as portions of spaghetti fall or nearly fall to the floor and plates are juggled, nearly dropped, caught, with musical accompaniment.)

Tony: And remember one thing. That is the last [of the spaghetti]. You work a the customer.

(Willy holds last undropped portion of spaghetti on plate, then looks tired, as does Chef Tony.) [In some versions, he did a neck-roll move which barely avoids spilling the spaghetti.]

Willy: I wish I could sit down first.
Tony (brings over small wooden chair, offers it to Willy): You sit down, cause I'm gonna take care of this customer.

(Willy puts plate of spaghetti on the chair. Tony starts to sit down, not seeing spaghetti there. Willy stops him. They argue about who's working the customer. While trying to emphasize a point, Willy accidentally lifts his leg up and stamps his foot down on the plate of spaghetti. As he holds his foot there, they both stare at it and realize the last of the spaghetti can't be served.)

Willy: I made another little boo boo.

(Tony silently weeps.)

Willy: Quick, Tony, some dessert. *(To distant customer):* You like some dessert? *(To Tony:)* Anything we got, it for the customer.
Tony: The pie? It's two days old.
Willy: The pie.

(Willy takes the cream pie out into the audience, looking for place to deliver it. Audience doesn't know exactly where the pie will end up.) [In some versions Willy would say, "I'm a got no job, I've a got nothing to lose." Then, in one version, Willy throws the pie into the face of a circus sound technician. In another version, it looks like an audience member will get pied, but instead it hits Tony in the face, and Tony chases Willy off, with music.]

5

Ramona the Tap-Dancing Gorilla
An Interview with Kimi Okada

KIMI OKADA performed as a tap-dancing gorilla named Ramona La Mona during the first season of the Pickle Family Circus. Her partner was Bill Irwin, also known as Humboldt the Clown, animal trainer. The duo gently mocked the bravado and cruelty of animal-taming acts.

Before joining the Pickles, Okada was a founding member and choreographer of the Oberlin Dance Collective, renamed ODC/SF after it moved from Oberlin College, Ohio (where Okada and Irwin first met), to San Francisco. Okada is presently the associate choreographer and director of the school at ODC. She has choreographed many dances for the company, including *Into the Inkwell* (1994) with former Pickle Family Circus clown Geoff Hoyle. Her 1988 ODC choreography for *Sauce for the Goose* was described by the *San Francisco Chronicle*, in terms fit for her artistry in the circus as well as outside it, as an "audacious circuslike romp" with "dancers [who] could well have been the clowns of the new vaudeville routines that also serve Okada so well."

This interview was conducted in San Francisco on August 18, 1998.

Several years after she introduced her tap-dancing gorilla to the Pickle Family Circus, Okada returned in 1983 to create the popular gorilla chorus line. Later duets were created for Lorenzo and Zaccio (Lorenzo Pisoni) in 1986; and she choreographed a clown dance for Pino, Queenie Moon, and Zaccio in 1989.

Since her circus days, Okada has continued to collaborate on dances with a number of clowns and comic actors, including Irwin, Hoyle, Robin Williams, and percussionist Keith Terry. In 1989, she was nominated for a Tony Award for best choreography (with co-choreographer Bill Irwin) on Broadway; the play nominated was *Largely New York*. Okada has also choreographed numbers for the San Francisco Mime Troupe, the Berkeley Repertory Theatre, the Los Angeles Theatre Center, the Los Angeles and Santa Fe Operas, and Julie Taymor's puppet epic, *Liberty's Taken*.

Bill [Irwin] and I were in the first Pickle Family show. They hired Bill as Willy the Clown. Then they found out that I was a dancer, and they needed a gorilla, so Ramona La Mona the tap-dancing gorilla was born.

I did the first two seasons with the Pickles as a dancing gorilla. Ironically, it was my first paying gig as a dancer. I had trained from high school on as a modern dancer. At ODC we weren't paid for anything at the time.

You did more than dance as the gorilla.

Bill was the trainer; I was the gorilla. The idea was that he made me do demeaning tricks: jump on a pogo stick, ride a bicycle, and then tap-dance. In the end, I one-upped him. The payoff was that I—or Ramona—was better than him as a dancer. No one knew I had tap shoes on until I started dancing.

It ended with silly show-tapping. I had never trained as a tap dancer, although I was always interested in it, because I was interested in rhythm. So I started tap dancing in my early twenties, which is late. I found it very difficult to be a tap-dancing gorilla, because I was from the postmodern school, where everything was formalist or abstract.

I remember going to my first circus rehearsal at the Mime Troupe studio; a lot of the Pickles were from the Mime Troupe. I was totally intimidated because I had to chase people around and beat my chest. It wasn't what I had been trained to do, but it was a lesson for me that it is okay to be silly.

Wasn't the act a contradiction in terms? A gorilla does not usually tap-dance gracefully.

No, and also I was not a very large gorilla, more like a large chimp. But I remember Larry Pisoni was fascinated by gorillas, and he wanted a gorilla in the show, although not a live animal. It was an animal-free circus.

When we performed in Chico in 108-degree weather, I had to pour ice down my suit. But it was fun, and I learned to dance in a popular form, quite different from my past experience.

Bill and I also did a ventriloquist act where I was the dummy and he was the ventriloquist who spoke gibberish German. It was almost the same premise as the gorilla act; the dummy is smarter than the ventriloquist. We did it at a benefit in the early '70s; it was never actually part of the circus.

Ramona La Mona (Kimi Okada) with her trainer (Bill Irwin). Photo by Terry Lorant.

How did you get from one gorilla to the gorilla chorus line?

From the beginning, Larry liked the idea of people in gorilla suits; it was funny, slightly intimidating, and appealing to children. Eight or nine years after the first gorilla act, Larry wanted to keep the tradition of the dancing gorilla in the circus. He asked me to choreograph a vaudevillesque clown dance for twelve gorillas, or however many there were. This time I was not one of the performers.

Original music was composed for the act. I asked for something upbeat, jazzy, silly. I pulled some images from early Hollywood line dances but with a slightly more sophisticated vocabulary. Busby Berkeley and Fred Astaire inspired me; but I had to remember [that] most of the Pickle performers were not necessarily dancers. Many of the circus performers weren't trained in dance, and they had a hard time learning it. When you have a gorilla suit on, it limits what you can do.

Was there a gorilla chorus scenario?

The setup was that one gorilla appeared, then another, then another. And incongruously, they started dancing. They ended up in unison. I think unison in this case is funny, especially if they're gorillas in unison. I was also playing with their being weighted down, having a low center of gravity, instead of jumping high.

No gorillas tap-dancing this time?

There was no tap-inspired step. That would have been too complicated; you need a wooden floor to hear a tap dancer, and the circus floor was canvas on top of a mat. (We had a special small wooden floor as a prop for me to dance on in the earlier gorilla act.) They strutted, did some tumbling, some falls, built a pyramid. They were big, furry, black; and then Lorenzo [son of Larry Pisoni] came out as a tiny gorilla; he looked very funny. And Larry (as Lorenzo Pickle, the clown) was the befuddled human among them. He was scared of them. He also realized the absurdity of the situation and tried to make the best of it. It ended up as a goof on a big show-biz, show-stopping dance—a parody of Broadway or Hollywood lines and formations.

I doubt that circus animals could have learned all those movements.

My experience with actors, physical comedians, people who are great improvisers, is that they have a terrible time learning steps and then remembering them. Bill and Geoff are brilliant dancers, but you can't get them to repeat the same thing twice. They have to work at it if they don't have the same physical recall as trained dancers. When I worked with Bill, Geoff, and Larry for the *Pickle Clown Reunion,* I remember just drilling, drilling, drilling.

You can also lose something with training. When you try to get a trained dancer to do something funny, it often isn't funny at all; the approach can be too technical. They're counting and asking, "How do I shift my weight?" Whereas when Bill [and] Geoff get up and improvise for two minutes, they come up with unbelievably spontaneous material.

There are advantages to working on dances with clowns.

There's delight in working with clowns. In my experience, there's an unfettered freedom that certain comedians—Bill, Geoff, Larry, and Robin Williams—bring from their experience with improvisation and working off of a crowd. There's creativity in that, which is exciting to work with. It's less

Kimi Okada rehearsing a dance with Derique McGee. Photo by Terry Lorant.

academic. There's a lack of control that is liberating in terms of finding a character, finding a solo, and finding something that turns physical dancing into brilliant comedy.

Also, from their work as comedians, they have acquired a very strong sense of character—particularly the wonderful clowns I've had the luxury of working with. It's different from doing modern dance; it's theatrically based. At least in the dances that I've done, there's the strength of the persona. Bill, for example, is very earnest and bumbling; he's trying to be dignified, pretending nothing is wrong, but in spite of what he does, he's always a fool. Geoff is much more wicked; he has a satiric edge.

They're always saying, "Let's do a funny move." But when you ask: "What's funny about it? Is it about the body rebelling?"

It often is.

It's often explained by a context that has to do with character, emotion, a situation which is innately funny or is a setup to be funny. In the *Pickle Clown Reunion* dance, for example, Bill and Geoff kept edging off the stage, and Larry kept falling in the pit; one of the jokes is that the choreography moves closer and closer to the edge of the stage. Not only is it funny moves, but there's a precarious side to the situation; he may fall off the stage. And there's an edge to it.

When you rehearse with the clowns, who comes up with the steps?

It depends on how much time I have. Sometimes, like in the reunion dance, I make up all the steps and teach them as a phrase, because we had limited time. When I did the "Monk Suite" with Geoff, we had more time, so we went into the studio, I turned on the video camera, and he improvised in front of it to Monk's music. And then I chose and wrote down some steps with names like the "noodle phrase" or the "electrified cat phrase," because we needed to come up with a vocabulary. We developed a lexicon of phrases or silly moves that we liked and strung them together to make a shaped piece. We did the same thing for "Cartoon."

Choreographing for the circus, you have to be big, you have to be flashy, you can't do subtle moves the way you can on a proscenium stage, where you can use facial expression and gesture more. Geoff's face is part of his body in a way that makes it very funny—which is not the case with many dancers.

Let me ask you about another circus dance. You choreographed Geoff and Larry's horned hat number?

They were renegades from a marching band, Elks, or brothers in a secret society. They had uniforms on and Buckingham Palace–style hats. I thought of them as being hapless renegades from some other group. Geoff had a bass drum, Larry had a tuba, and they put them down to dance. Although I'm not old enough to have seen vaudeville, it was my imagining of what a vaudeville dance would look like: lots of straight-legged slapping of the feet and quirky moves. It was a duo of two guys messing around in those hats. They kept the hats on. I was trying to cull from an older popular form, which I've always been interested in with my group choreography for the circus.

You also developed a comic dance with Geoff Hoyle and Robin Williams.

Yes, it was "Yep Roc Hersey" with Slim Gaylord singing a Middle Eastern menu. It sounds like gibberish, but actually an Arabic menu was the text. I'm very fond of Slim Gaylord's music. I found this music and it was so "out there." We decided to do the dance of two waiters who were out of their minds. I made up the movement, because we had very little time to work with Robin, who, by the way, has incredible recall. He remembers everything. I was astonished by how much movement he retained. Anyway, the dance was all about waiters in tuxedos, with towels over their hands, doing silly moves. The movement was based on serving and being servile. Once again I drew from a popular vocabulary, and the ideas led to all these silly moves about carrying trays. They were slightly fey, but not obviously so, and very obsequious and crazed, the kind of characters which Geoff and Robin could do without any difficulty.

Part of the humor arises from the audience having no idea what the words mean.

Yes, and it doesn't matter at all. After a couple of hours of rehearsal, I was weak from laughing so much; the two of them would just go off. They invented a lot. Comedians are very mimetic; they have such good eyes and ears for seeing, hearing, and copying. And they create narrative. There's one moment when they're in a canoe. Geoff is in the front paddling, and Robin is in back, smoking a cigarette; it lasts only a second and then it's gone, a fleeting image. Then they have a fake sheep and a duck, quick silly things.

We don't often see these comic dances in dance repertoires or in circuses.

It's rare because you need brilliant performers who can play characters and physical comedy, like Geoff, Larry, Bill, Robin. If you showed the waiter dance's steps to a trained dancer, he or she might be able to do it, but it wouldn't be nearly as funny. There are some wonderful eccentric dancers who are loose-limbed, rubber-legged, and innately funny, with a quirky sense of timing. But you can't simply say you're going to make a funny dance; the dance has to be *about* something, like an individual versus a group, or about someone who's lost in some world, or about a relationship between two people. Then with timing, narrative, and character, it might be funny.

Funny things include any kind of rebellion in the body—where something doesn't work the way you want it (Bill and Geoff do that a lot)—and incongruity and juxtaposition contrasting one kind of movement against another, something huge next to a little comic aside.

You had contrasts of that sort between the ensemble and Bill in Largely New York.

Bill brought me in to work with the ensemble, to formalize it as a self-conscious, kind of post-postmodern group, all dressed in black and doing inexplicable, arbitrary things. My background in postmodern dance made this familiar territory.

You were making fun of the postmoderns and your own forms?

Yes, that's what Bill wanted. I was certainly up for that, too. And since I knew it so well, it wasn't hard to do. It was a parody of dance taking itself too seriously and the dancer who says: "Excuse me, I'm following a form here."

You created a satire of dance—can we call it an anti-dance dance?

I would say that coming from the dance world, having spent so much time in the dance world and seen so much of it, my tolerance for bad dance is low. For me, there's nothing worse than going to a bad dance concert, and I've been to many. Parody is one way of responding and showing respect or love for the art. It's kind of a left-handed tribute.

Earlier you mentioned "eccentric dance." That was a term used to describe vaudeville dancers earlier in the century.

I've seen little clips of incredible rubber-legged and peg-legged danc-ers, unbelievably weird dances done by incredibly adept performers. It's very poorly documented.

Bill has done dances that seem to draw on the "eccentric" genre. So have you, in your choreography.

I think street dancing (break dancing) is probably the closest dancers come to it today. Contortionists do something like it in the circus. There have always been brave dancers who do weird things, but there's no forum for them anymore. Where would you do it, except maybe on the street?

You also created outdoor dances (if not street dances) as a choreographer for the San Francisco Mime Troupe.

My work with them has been less about comic dancing than about ad-vancing the story line through movement. The first time I did dances for them was in *Spain 36* [a play about the Spanish Civil War] with the L.A. Theatre Company. The most successful one was a revolutionary dance for the people of Barcelona, a call to arms, a very rhythmic dance with rifles; it was about solidarity and finding power with numbers. It wasn't a comic dance at all. Another dance in *Spain* was a stuffy minuet for heads of state: Churchill, Tojo, Stalin.

The dances in *Offshore* [a play about Pacific Rim trade] were all based on Asian theatre and music forms (Chinese opera, Kabuki, Taiko drumming).

Recently Dan Chumley [director of the Mime Troupe], Ed Holmes [actor in the Mime Troupe], and I have been doing some work with car-toon animators. We teach movement workshops for animators in their stu-dios. But you can't teach "funny"; you can only teach tools of getting there.

But these cartoonists need your assistance?

Well, we think they do. They are technological wizards. They can make any object dance and do whatever they want. I couldn't have some-one stay up in the air for ten seconds and do a triple flip; they can. But they need a sense of comic timing or dramatic character, or the relationship of one character to another, which would make something funny. For starfish to dance and be engaging, it requires all the elements you have when two people dance.

The animators have great imaginations [and] are highly creative; but they have no training in things which are the basis of theatre and dance. They have to go back to the basics of performance. So it's good (for them and for us) that they're hiring us. It's ironic that at this point in my career I'm choreographing for cartoon characters. At least they'll do whatever you want; you don't have any problems with the performers.

Queenie Moon

An Interview with Joan Mankin

JOAN MANKIN joined the Pickle Family Circus in its second season as the clown Queenie Moon with Donald Forrest (as Ralph Deliberate) as her partner. Queenie and Ralph left the Pickles to perform with San Francisco's Make-a-Circus in the same year. In 1988, the duo returned to the Pickles. In 1989 and 1990, Mankin performed with a new partner, Diane Wasnak, known in the ring as Pino. They were the only female clown duo featured in the world of circus at that time, according to historian and director Judy Finelli.

When not with the Pickles, Mankin performed with some of the San Francisco Bay Area's most innovative and popular theatre ensembles, including the San Francisco Mime Troupe, the Eureka Theatre, and Lilith Women's Theater. She also appeared with the Dell'Arte Players, the Aurora Theatre Company, and the American Conservatory Theatre and in the San Francisco and California Shakespeare Festivals. In recent years, she has also acted in the company she cofounded, Miracle Theatre.

This interview was conducted in San Francisco on October 6, 1998.

Did your five years with the San Francisco Mime Troupe prepare you for clowning with the Pickles?

That's where I learned juggling, with Larry Pisoni. Then I met Donald Forrest in New York, when the Mime Troupe went there with *The Dragon Lady's Revenge*. Donald wanted to become part of the Mime Troupe and was very interested in juggling. So he moved back to San Francisco. He had been a struggling actor in New York, and he wanted to become a struggling actor here. We started juggling together with my brother, Danny, on the street; in our performances, we interspersed comedy skits with juggling. We were "Boris, Morris, and Dolores." Then we became the "Bay City Reds," and the act was much more about formation juggling, less about comedy. The Bay City Reds juggling troupe included Wendy Parkman [later a trapeze artist with the Pickles], Billy Kessler [later a Pickle Circus acrobat], Merle Goldstone [from the Mime Troupe], Daniel Mankin, Donald, and me.

When the Pickle Family Circus needed someone to take Bill Irwin's place for the part of the year he couldn't be there, they had auditions. Donald and I did the audition like we were drunk clowns, as I remember it; but our audition didn't have much to do with what we did in the show. Donald was the one who thought of my name, Queenie Moon. (Queenie had been my name as a little girl; but he thought of putting "Moon" at the end of it.) And then he became Ralph Deliberate.

We did one act as Queenie and Ralph *before* we auditioned for the Pickles. My sister outlaw [not yet an in-law] was getting married to a man from India, and for their party we did a clown version of the *Kama Sutra*, with all those different sexual positions on a bed in front of their somewhat straitlaced Indian friends. That was the beginning of Queenie and Ralph.

We developed two main acts for the 1976 Pickles show. One of them centered around cooking a chicken dinner. It was very "politically correct," too, because I was a worker in overalls. We were trying to break down role models. It was all based on the idea of men taking on more of the work that women were supposed to do.

That was the period when I was working in the shipyards, after I left the Mime Troupe in 1975. In the Mime Troupe we had been doing all these shows about the proletariat, and I had no idea what the proletariat was; I didn't have work experience. So I walked into the Bethlehem Steel ship-yard office the day after a federal mandate arrived saying they had to hire women. They hired me as a journeyperson and set me out on the ships right away. Of course, they never gave me any training; it was a token thing. But I wanted to find out what it was like, and there was a group of women who had been there since the war. The clown act grew out of my experience there as well as [with] the Mime Troupe.

In the clown act, I came home from work, and we got into an argument about who was going to cook dinner. He said he would, and the clown act was about Ralph trying to cook a chicken. It was a rubber chicken, of course.

The Pickles never used live (or once live) animals in their acts. Was Queenie talking him through his cooking?

Yes, I would give him instructions. I would say *[voice changes to squeaky, high pitch here]*: "Beat the egg!" and he would smash it. Then: "Coat the chicken!" Then he put up a little coat and put it on the chicken. Then he put it in the oven, and the oven blew up. That was his favorite part; he loved doing pyrotechnics. I remember sitting there as Queenie, feeling very smug about the mess Ralph was making.

We also had a song and dance in the act. *[Sings:]* "Learn what you need, share what you know, do a deed, begin to read, make life grow. If I ask a lot of questions, don't get sore. I've never done this thing before. It takes a long time to do things right. A house isn't built overnight." It was specifically for the kids. The idea was that if you don't know how to do something, you should try to learn it.

*That's a funny voice Queenie has. The critic Nancy Scott once called it "the squeakiest voice in northern California" when she praised your "maniacal cook." *Ralph and Queenie's Kitchen *was more of a direct response to political and gen-der issues of the '70s than many other Pickle clown acts, I think.*

Most of the circus acts weren't political comedy, but their roots were very much based in the politics of that time. The circus had community group sponsors, and many of the groups were independent, progressive schools set up and run by people who were influenced by the Mime Troupe. They definitely used the same community. Of course, the circus wasn't as political as the Mime Troupe, because, thankfully, Larry [Pisoni] didn't want to have the circus be too dogmatic or theoretical. He and Peggy didn't have that need; but the ethos was definitely something from the '70s.

What were some of your other acts in the 1976 season?

Donald and I were also involved in *The Big Juggle* at the end of the show. Our other clown act was a carpenter act, which involved wooden boards. You're holding the board on your shoulders; you swing it around and just barely miss the other person. Most of it had me doing the turns and him doing the acrobatics, jumping over and tumbling under the board. But again it traded on the idea of women doing work which customarily was done by men.

How did Queenie look, for those who didn't see her in person?

She changed. In 1976 she was much more proletarian, with extra-big, baggy, blue-striped overalls and a flowered shirt, a red nose, whiteface. I wore work shoes and a hardhat.

No wig, just your own curly red hair?

I've always worn my own hair. I need a wig for real life, to cover up my clown hair. She got a new nose in 1988. (Donald designed it.) And as time went on, Queenie became more of a *femme* clown, in flouncy dresses and coats with lots of flowers, very frilly, with beautiful red pointy boots. It was a funny opposition to Pino, who's so different, the furthest from *femme*. Queenie was definitely *femme,* and Pino was definitely butch, almost like a man when she wore a suit. For Queenie, it was a celebration; she reveled in being feminine to excess. She's a very fully realized character. I have other characters in comedy, but she's the clown. If I were going to do a clown show in the theatre, like *Fool Moon,* she would be the one who would come out.

But the show would have to be called Queenie Moon, *not* Fool Moon. *So you've kept this clown alive, in your repertoire, over twenty years now.*

I'd have to say it's closer to fifty years, because Queenie was my name when I was a little girl, and I was kind of a clown when I was a kid. But in another sense, too, she has stayed with me; she is a very full expression of a part of me, as clowns are the deepest part of people who create them. She's right there, in my best moments, hooked into that life force.

Robert Hurwitt once called Queenie "a riotously obnoxious extrovert." I think he meant it as a compliment.

I'd say it's very accurate. She's very obnoxious, and the squeaky voice really adds to that. She got more obnoxious as time went on.

Queenie Moon also misuses words. She's not intentionally destroying the English language, is she?

No, she thinks of herself as quite erudite, quite knowledgeable about things, and she's not. Her sense of the language and how to use it is a little bit warped. She was the "Ringmattress," for example. Jon Carroll wrote quite a bit of the dialogue in 1989. I remember one speech he wrote for her. *[In Queenie's squeaky, high-pitched voice:]* "The circus is many things to many people. It is the daring of the acrobats. The dextralambiguitry of the jugglers. The smile of a small child. But most of all the circus is ME! QUEENIE MOON!" Jon Carroll and I worked on that together. "Dextralambiguitry" is a perfect example of her language.

Although Queenie is a juggling clown, there's not that much physical shtick associated with Queenie. She's a verbal clown. Also, she doesn't function so well on her own. She's a very good "Ringmattress," a very good master of ceremonies, a character who likes to be bossy. But it's hard to be bossy when there's no one there. Her clown character needs other clowns around her to function.

When Queenie and Ralph returned to the Pickle Family Circus in 1988, you both came out of the audience. The ringmaster, Lorenzo Pisoni, first announced that the circus was missing its clowns and would choose guests from the audience by lottery to serve as that evening's clowns.

Working with Judy Finelli [director of the circus that season], we came up with the concept that we had known each other in another lifetime and met by chance when we got pulled out of the audience because of the numbers on our tickets. The notion of past life experiences proved too complex, but it was very funny when we just came out of the audience and became clowns.

It also acknowledged that some new (or at least not recently seen) clowns were appearing that season, after Lorenzo Pickle had departed. You did new acts that year?

We tried for the longest time to do a musical clown act and never got that together. I did a hypnotism act during different parts of the summer. We did the plank act. I did a magic act with Stephen LaBounty, who was an apprentice with the circus. What I remember fondly was the juggling act we did with John Gilkey and Tash Wesp. That was a wonderful act, my favorite juggling act. Tash and John looked 1950s, and the idea was that Donald and I didn't know how to juggle, and they taught us, to '50s music. It was beautifully choreographed by Judy. And then we did *Café des Artistes*.

That was quite a change in the Pickles repertoire. Café des Artistes *was inspired by the "restaurant jugglers" who created* An Animated Supper Chez Maxim's *in 1910.*

Yes, Judy [Finelli] took her concept from that act. Arnie Zazlov came in as a director and helped us develop it. The idea behind it was to tell a story and to have everyone in the circus integrated into the story. I think that it was far ahead of its time, and right for the Pickles to do, because it was an ensemble production. *Café des Artistes* was a continuation of the ensemble circus, in which all of us set up and all of us struck the circus, without a separation between technicians and performers; we were all working in it together.

The café in the act also was a place where everyone could be an artist; everyone there could do something special.

Yes, the people were sitting in the restaurant, eating, and then all of a sudden they would become circus artists. I played a character who was different from Queenie. She was a woman who came into the restaurant with her daughter. Donald was the maître d'. It didn't have the same potential for developing specific clown pieces; you had to fit into the arc of the piece, which led to the trapeze act on the chandelier. A busboy in the restaurant and a customer got together on the trapeze. That's what we were working toward, and along the way we had to fit in the hand balancing act, a rolla bolla act, and juggling of champagne bottles. In that piece, Donald and I were more comic actors or comic characters than clowns. And the other performers had to do more acting. It was a stretch for everyone, and it evolved tremendously over the two seasons it was done. In the second season, 1989, Diane Wasnak played the role of the young thief, I was the cook, the plot changed, the acts changed, and the piece was renamed *Café Chaotique.*

Do you think the idea of doing circus acts in a narrative for Café des Artistes *led to the next Pickles production,* La La Luna Sea?

Definitely. It led to making the entire circus, not just the second half, tell a story. Within *Luna Sea* I had more of a chance to be Queenie, and I enjoyed that. It was difficult because Judy had brought in several new people to work on it. She brought in Tandy Beal, Peter Brosius, and Lu Yi. They were working together on something which had never been done before by other circuses; and they themselves had never worked with one another. Also Judy had been diagnosed the year before with MS, and her endurance for work as artistic director was reduced.

I felt that the performers were left out of the process. That had not been the case before. The important thing about working as a clown in the Pickles was that you really had a voice in the shaping of the circus. The circus developed around the clowns. The clowns were critical in the sensibility of each show, and there was always room for that. It was a clown-sensitive circus. It was a "clown love zone." "Clowns Welcome Here!"

Now that I look back on it, I see that when we worked on *Café des Artistes* and *Café Chaotique,* it was the beginning of a situation that was not clown-determined. Then we got to *Luna Sea,* and although Diane and I were the protagonist and antagonist of the piece (Queenie's theft of the saxophone started the whole thing going), in another sense we were merely clowns in a much larger picture.

I think the best clowning comes when you don't have to follow a line. You can go where you want to go, take something where your characters take you, as in *commedia lazzi,* and not have to be faithful to a narrative.

So there are some disadvantages—as least as far as clowns are concerned—in the longer narrative form of circus. Maybe shorter acts, fifteen- to twenty-minute entrées, would be preferable? You might have more freedom as a clown in those small, self-contained acts.

You know, clowns are anarchistic by nature, and when you've got anarchists—clowns—who are forced to go along with the plot, then you're working against the nature of the clown. Now there are advantages to the longer form; I think it's a wonderful experience for an audience to see the connections and the arc in the story. I think by the end of the 1990 season, at [San Francisco's] Palace of Fine Arts, *Luna Sea* had a lot of magic to the story; that was very positive. Also, I like experimenting and bringing theatricality into the circus, even if things get lost along the way.

Pino and Queenie were able to clown around in Luna Sea *anyway?*

Yes, the opening section, which sets up the story, is a clown act. We find the saxophone in the case and I start to play it. Then we open up the piano [and] get inside it; it's a bed, and we do this whole act inside the piano, trying to go to sleep. Then I steal the saxophone. That was fun. But there was a certain way in which the process alienated me. It took me a long time to feel vested in the piece.

Queenie Moon (Joan Mankin, *left*) with Pino (Diane Wasnak). Photo by Terry Lorant.

You and Diane did some other, more independently created clown acts before Luna Sea, *in the 1989 season. There was one where Diane arrived in a baby carriage?*

Yes, after I introduced the show as the Ringmattress, Karen Quest came up with a baby carriage and said, "Would you watch my baby? I've got to run." So I had to watch this baby from hell; her name was Electra. She had a baby bottle, which she kept throwing out. My job was to introduce the show, but here I had to take care of this baby. I was trying to keep her quiet. She took bites out of the carriage and jumped up and down in there. (We had a kind of minitrampoline inside.) The carriage tipped over. She climbed out of the carriage into the audience, and I had to chase her around. Then I ran and got this big balloon for her, to keep her quiet. The balloon went out into the audience, and that was how the show started.

Diane is livid because we did our act in 1989, and now in Las Vegas, Cirque du Soleil's *Mystère* starts with the baby throwing the balloon out. Diane's in that act, but in a less creative situation.

My favorite part of our act came after I chased the baby through the audience. I'd finally get her back onstage, and she'd pull my skirt off, and I would say *[in Queenie's high-pitched, very loud voice]*: "OH, YOU INAPPRO-PRIATE CHILD!" The audience liked that—it was so New Age. It was a wonderful opening act.

That year we did another clown act I loved, *Saxophones.* It started out with me coming out by the band, snapping my fingers, and saying *[in Queenie's high voice]*: "Hey Dude, let's preserve." Harvey Robb would stop the band and say: "Queenie, do you mean, let's jam?" I would say, "What is it, Harvey?" And he would say, "Do you mean, 'What it is?'" Then I would start to play the saxophone, in my own way. Pino came out in her short jacket and hat, Chaplin-like, and started playing a polka on her accordion. I would turn to her and make a gesture which implied, "Square, get lost." She would come back with a tuba, start to play, and I'd make the same gesture. She came in with a violin and started to play bluegrass. I took the violin away. She came back on with a saxophone. We started to play a saxophone duet, except that her sax wouldn't make any sound, so I'd pull out a pair of jumper cables and jump-start her sax from mine. Then Lorenzo [Pisoni] came out in a gorilla suit, with a saxophone, and the three of us did a dance. Kimi Okada choreographed it.

You don't see concerts like that in a symphony hall, or even in the circus anymore—a great loss. Since you left the Pickles, has the circus clowning you did there influenced your work as an actor?

Yes, I could never go backwards from being a clown. I could never *not* draw on it. But there aren't that many opportunities where my particular clown has a venue, so I have to use it in other ways. For instance, I'm working now in a production of *The Lower Depths*, by Gorky, where I play a street person. I decided she should wear very large shoes, almost like clown shoes, because I saw a street person with shoes five sizes too large. I was immediately drawn to that look, because it is a clown look.

The Pickle Family Circus has had so many accomplished and popular clowns since it began. Did you ever see any of them as your rivals?

No, maybe that was my problem. *[Laughter.]* Both Judy and Peggy were interested in developing women as clowns. When Diane and I were performing, we were the only female clown duo in the world performing in a circus, according to Judy. There's always a woman who's the partner of the man; but it was a breakthrough to have two women be the head clowns. I was very fortunate to be able to work with Diane, because she's a dedicated and integrated clown. She thinks in clown terms, totally physical. If I had been working with someone else who came from an acting background in the same the way I did, I think it would have been more difficult to make that breakthrough.

That time being a clown in the Pickle Family Circus was so satisfying artistically, and in every way. I remember our truck once pulled onto a field in Tucson, Arizona, where we had played the year before, and all these kids came out and asked, "Where's Queenie?"

And what did you reply?

[In loud, high-pitched voice:] "SHE'S HAVING HER HAIR DONE; SHE'LL BE HERE SOON!" No, but that was such a satisfying thing. That's not to say I would mind Steven Spielberg asking the same thing:

"Where's Joan, because I'm dying to make a movie with her?" But on its own level, that was the apex in Tucson, a tremendously rewarding and fulfilling thing, for kids to have that character become so much a part of them that they remembered a year later and were asking about her. That was a wonderful thing about the circus; you really felt that people took it into their hearts and felt they were part of it.

Ralph Deliberate

An Interview with Donald Forrest

DONALD FORREST joined the Pickle Family Circus as the clown Ralph Deliberate in the summer of 1976. He and his clown partner, Queenie Moon, performed for Make-a-Circus later the same year. They returned to the Pickles to perform clown acts together again in the 1988 season. Before joining the circus, Forrest had been an acrobat in Dr. Quackenbush's Travelling Medicine Show, an actor off and on Broadway in New York, and a juggler with the Bay City Reds. He also performed with the San Francisco Mime Troupe. He is currently co–artistic director of the Dell'Arte Players and has been an actor and co-creator of plays with the company since 1978.

What led you to join the Pickles in 1976?

My mom had been an acrobat, so as an actor I always had an interest in acrobatics and juggling. The San Francisco Mime Troupe came to New York and played in the theatre where I had been performing a play called *The*

This interview took place in San Francisco on October 17, 1998, just before Forrest and the other Dell'Arte Players performed their newest play, *Mad Love,* at a festival in Venezuela.

Dirtiest Show in Town. I had been rotated out of the show when they played *The Dragon Lady's Revenge* at the Astor Place Theatre. I volunteered in their box office. I fell in love with that show. That style was an amalgam of a lot of the physical theatre and skills that I inherited from my mom, and yet it had some acting values. So I kind of attached myself to the Mime Troupe, and in another way I attached myself to Joan Mankin.

Within a year or so, I had driven out to California on a motorcycle and auditioned for the Mime Troupe. But it had changed. Larry Pisoni, Michael Christensen, and Paul Binder, who had been juggling, were not in positions of power anymore. They had been encouraging me to come out. As a white male, I was not offered membership in the company.

I was brash and undaunted. I developed a street juggling act, called the Bay City Reds. It included Merle Goldstone, Joan Mankin, [and] her brother Danny Mankin. Then some other people came in and out of it: Jeff Raz, Diane Perry, Billy Kessler, Wendy Parkman. There was a Mime Troupe gang at the center of it. Early on in 1973, Merle and I took a tour to Mexico to visit a theatre company there, Los Mascarones. We ended up staying there several months, working with the company in Mexico City. The tradition of the clown in Mexico was a big influence on me.

Joan and I also worked with Adrian Vargas's Chicano company, Teatro de la Gente, in San Jose. It was an offshoot of Teatro Campesino, and I started to develop a clown who was a sharp dresser, not a helpless bum, for the juggling act. I had creases sewn into my white pressed dungarees. I had seen all these clowns who were victims, stumblers, and I wanted to have a clown who was an ace in his own little world. I wanted him to appeal to the kids in my neighborhood and the people I had played to in Mexico. People called it a *Cholo* clown, kind of like El Pachucho.

I wanted to play someone who was oblivious to the juggling, who might wander through the act. I tried it out in Union Square [and] other places; but I found that if you got quiet and sensitive, the tourists would walk away. So my character became very bombastic, like a young Jackie Gleason with a mustache. He's the guy who yells really loud and then gets hit by a plank while the innocent is bending over.

You created this clown's character before you joined the Pickles?

All the elements were there. I didn't have the character name [Ralph Deliberate]. I worked with Larry a little bit on traditional clowning. He was looking for someone who would be an *elegante* and would look nice. In putting the clowns together, Larry had asked Joan and me to explore one clown who would be an *auguste*, a simpler clown, and one clown who would be pompous. It was where I had wanted to go with our juggling act. But it was clear we weren't going to be the jugglers; that act was already reserved.

You developed several clown acts during the 1976 season with the Pickles. One was a plank routine?

We had worked very hard to present a skill act—skillful clowns. I was the master carpenter and Queenie was an apprentice. We built a plank and we borrowed licks from Chaplin and Keaton, where the plank would fall and narrowly miss. She would pick up the plank and hold it on her shoulder. She couldn't see me when I called her. She would swing and turn. It allowed me to do some falling.

It required a lot of attention from the audience, and we worked on ways to focus their attention on the precision. We finished it by completing a teeter-totter. I had a phony board and it would crack. I came out with another board, a heavy one. Joan would sit on it, I would sit, she would go up about two feet and she couldn't bring it down. She then would go out into the audience and get four or five kids. The board would rise to a neutral position, then she would jump on the end, and it would shoot me off in a somersault. It was fun and traditional and involved some acrobatics.

You also created Ralph and Queenie's Kitchen *for the 1976 season?*

Yes, in a rehearsal at The Farm [a center for artists in San Francisco]. I had built a couple of props: an oven, a pipe wrench, a chicken, a homemade flashpot. We had an ending already—a blowout—since I had the flashpot.

The conceit of the act was that the clowns had already been seen working (in the plank act). Now we had the same clowns coming home from work. We had a little drop cloth, painted to look like black and white linoleum, because we knew we were going to make a mess.

I should describe what the clowns looked like. Joan's clown had an old pair of dungarees, funny leggings, and she insisted on wearing two left work boots, which ruined her. She wore a traditional clown ball mask of energy right on the front of her nose, and her own bright red, whacked-out hair. Lots of color in her face, with blue eyebrows, like Lou Jacobs. She'd work for an hour on this makeup, and when she was all done I'd joke that it looked just like her.

My clown had a pure white face with a white bald cap. The features included a black lower lip, black vertical lines in the eyes, [and] a black top-knot piece of hair that went straight up into the air and was sewn to the bald cap. That was covered by a white cone hat. I had a yellow Banlon shirt and creased white overalls. I was very well dressed, meticulous.

My character was kind of a know-it-all. But when the clowns got into their home, Joan and I wanted to break down the roles where I was the master and she was the apprentice. The text of the cooking act was loud and had some traditional clowning that we could handle. Joan and I both have really big voices.

That clown, Ralph, looked weird, walked weird. I always wore white gloves, and my two index fingers were always pointed like that guy who says, "Aliens must register every month," his thumbs are always out. He looked like Mercury the Winged Messenger.

In 1988, Ralph and Queenie returned to the Pickle Family Circus. You performed in Café des Artistes *that year.*

Judy Finelli had a great vision we weren't able to realize, because it was production-strong and required musical concepts that moved away from jazz, and the band and the leader were not comfortable with it. The conceit of the show was that the first act would be a succession of skill acts, each one more archaic than the last: a contemporary setting, then an acrobatic act from the '60s, then a juggling act from the '50s. One of the clown acts was based on a song, "When and Where," from the '30s. It needed costumes and a lot of musical ambience to support it. It was hard for the band to break out of its progressive jazz mode.

So it went back in time, toward the turn of the century. The opening of the second act was the turn-of-the-century event where Ralph and Queenie fell in love. There was a constant theme of déjà vu through the first act, a theme of "I know you from somewhere. Where was it?" Then we see them meet in the café.

*In the second act, you weren't the clown Ralph, you were a different charac-
ter, a café manager.*

It was a hard breaking of the rules of clowning, and I would have to say
that it was not successful. Once you introduce a clown, he has certain rules
and a world of his own, and it shouldn't change. The conceit that I laid out
just now was not clear. Had it been clear, going back in time to that point,
then you could have had that first incarnation of Ralph as bombastic and
boisterous, which was what the *Café des Artistes* skit required. It required the
maître d' to be overbearing in order to throw focus to different performers
who filled the ring. The characters needed more support for that to work.
We had trouble with focus in the second act.

Joan and I had signed on after Judy, Peggy, and Terry [Lorant] took us
to lunch and said, "We've got an idea, and here it is: The clowns go back in
time; they can't remember when they met." I was entranced by it. I just wish

Joan Mankin and Donald Forrest in *Café des Artistes* costumes. Photo by Terry Lorant.

all the other people on the team—the technicians, the designers, and the musical director—could have been at that lunch. If we had all gotten on with the same show, it would have been dazzling.

There are a number of groups, a number of people, who have tried to create this hybrid of circus and theatre. Judy Finelli was talking the talk, and I got goose bumps when I was imagining how this might work. I was imagining an evening at the circus where the clowns were woven into the acrobatic act, the juggling act, the charivari [the beginning act], to tell a story that had a beginning, middle, and end, and that it would be a journey. A year later we saw Cirque du Soleil with their show, and sure enough, it was a group of people going on a journey. The Pickles's plan, in my imagination, was more substantial, because it had to do with the feelings of unrequited love that the characters had for one another. The characters had an appetite, a need for something that they didn't understand; it was a delicious concept.

In the Mime Troupe, we had all these ideas that it's important, politically correct, for characters to realize where they're at and to metamorphose. The character should change. But in my experience in clowning, I realized that once you put on a mask, or clown makeup, that's who you are; it doesn't change. Clowns can influence the world around them to evolve or metamorphose, but the clowns remain constant.

I thought I had a chance to realize that in *Café des Artistes,* so you would see that the maître d' was the liminal ancestor of Ralph. But it didn't work; it was just a new guy coming on with the same nose.

You once spoke about a Pickle "tradition of great clowning from Bill to Geoff to Larry." Do you, or did you, see yourself as part of that tradition?

There was a tradition there. I have to say that although I had some of the right physical skills, I'm mainly an actor. I did my best, and I'm proud of the work. I especially liked the integration of the clowns as acrobats in the first act of *Café.* I was able to make the most of my (at that time) thirty-eight-year-old body, to still be the bottom of the three-high and carry out routines with character; that was great.

But now you prefer to act in plays?

I had been a juggler and a clown for about five years when we did a play by Stan Laurel, *Birds of a Feather,* at Dell'Arte in 1978 on an indoor legit stage. It was all character-based, based on attitudes. I got out on stage and people were laughing. They were already looking at you. They weren't looking at birds or the band or children getting cotton candy stuck on their faces. The focus was there; the lights were on you. I just couldn't believe how easy it was if you didn't have to keep the damn clubs up in the air!

Ralph and Queenie's Kitchen

A Clown Act by Donald Forrest and Joan Mankin

R ALPH WALKS *in the door. He hangs his hat on a coat rack, but it has a garage door spring on it. When he puts his hat on the spring, it bends over; then he lets his hand go, and it catapults the hat into the house. He puts a couple of things on it and throws the stuff into the house or into the Pickle Family Circus Band seated nearby.*

Then Queenie enters. She hangs her hat and it stays there. She takes off something else and it hangs there. Then she takes off her nose and hangs it on the coat rack. She takes three steps and then, "AGGHH! AGGHHH!" she grabs her throat like Ralph should perform some Heimlich. He looks at her for a second, tries to do CPR, then gives her back her nose, and she goes, "AHH!" and breathes again.

Then Queenie opens a tiny little beer and goes, "sip, sip, sip, ah." [Olympia has seven-ounce cans.] Then Ralph opens a king-size Miller and squeezes it so hard that a stream of foam shoots to the rafters. [In a wind it would get all over the audience or the band.]

Queenie opens another tiny beer, "sip, sip, sip," and another big beer explodes on Ralph. Finally he gives her one of the big cans. She is ready to open it, but Ralph takes it back. There is a toy snake coiled up in it, and Ralph screams when it flies out. Then Ralph puts the can down.

> *Ralph (in a deep voice):* I'm hungry.
> *Queenie (in a high-pitched voice):* Me too!
> *Ralph:* Well, why don't you cook dinner?
> *Queenie:* Why don't you?
> *Ralph (very proud of himself):* Because I don't know how!
> *Queenie (as she rises, the band rises with her, and she loudly says):* Well, it's time you learned!

(The clowns go out to the front with the band. Queenie asks for an opening note, and band leader Barry Glick hits a little triangle.)

> *Queenie (to band leader):* Thanks, Barry.
> *(Queenie and Ralph sing, with band accompaniment):*

> If you know how to tie your shoes,
> teach your little sister the knot you use.
> Do you know how to whistle, or how to feed the cat?
> Maybe your friend would like to learn that.
> Can you climb a tree, can you ride a bike,
> could you teach those tricks to me?
> Learn what you need, share what you know.
> Do a deed, begin to read, make life grow.
> If I ask a lot of questions, don't get sore.
> I've never done this thing before.
> It takes a long time to do things right.
> A house isn't built overnight.

(Chorus of "Learn what you need," etc., is repeated. Then they stop; the band goes back to its stand.)

> *Queenie (to band leader):* Thanks, Barry. That was hip.

(Queenie opens a big cookbook and reads aloud.)

Queenie: Chicken fricassee. Step one. Beat the egg.

(Ralph tosses an egg into the air, catches it, smashes it in his fist; it splatters horizontally.)

Queenie (patiently): No, no, no.

(She carefully takes an egg out, drops it in a big tin bowl, and beats the hell out of it with a big metal spoon. The band shakes as she stirs it up.)

Queenie: Step two. Coat the chicken.

(Ralph takes a rubber chicken, throws it in the air, catches it, puts a little coat on it.)

Queenie: No, no, no.

(Queenie takes out some flour, which flies everywhere as she rattles it all around with the egg and chicken. As this point, Peggy Pickle [Snider], in curlers and babushka because she is dressing for her next juggling act, enters and screams: "Butter!" A wet, yellow bar of soap is squeezed in turn by everyone and flies into the air.)

Queenie: Crush the pepper.

(Sneezing bout begins.)

Queenie: Now bake the chicken.

(Ralph turns on the gas. The clowns look everywhere for a match. When they find one, kids in the audience begin to say, "Don't do it. Don't light the match.")

Ralph puts his head in the oven as he lights the match. The flashpot blows, a small explosion erupts, and Queenie and Peggy Pickle chase Ralph off as the smoke drifts over the house.)

Ms. Wombat

An Interview with Andrea Snow

ANDREA SNOW toured with the Pickle Family Circus during the 1979 season. Her clown character, Ms. Wombat, performed acts with Lorenzo Pickle and Mr. Sniff. Before and after joining the Pickles, she was an actress with the San Francisco Mime Troupe and was featured in many plays, performing as the Dragon Lady in *The Dragon Lady's Revenge* and Factperson in *Factperson*.

Why did you wait until 1979 to join the Pickles?

I replaced Bill Irwin! *[Laughter.]* That was a joke. Obviously, I couldn't replace him. I was just the new clown after Bill left. Larry Pisoni and I were friends, and he invited me to join for the season, April to September. It included a great tour in northern California, Oregon, and Alaska. By mid-September, Alaska was so cold that I couldn't sleep in my tent. The permafrost was only three inches below the surface. So the state fair people found an old pigeon coop where I slept well off the ground on a little cot.

How did Ms. Cornelia Wombat come into existence?

She was the clown character I created for the *Sandsniff* act with Geoff.

This interview was conducted in San Francisco on October 23, 1998.

She was an eccentric and an amateur ornithologist, out in the field looking for the elusive "sandsniff."

It just so happens that Mr. Sniff, with his extremely large nose, is on the beach, wearing trunks and flippers, and she mistakes him for the sandsniff. She pursues him with her butterfly net, chasing him into the ocean where he almost drowns. She rescues him and discovers that he's a man, and she promptly falls in love. He's horrified and runs, and she continues pursuing him. Here we have opposing impulses: Ms. Wombat's obsession with an object of desire and Mr. Sniff's aversion to friendly human contact.

Where did Ms. Wombat's name come from?

A wombat is an Australian animal, and the word attracted me. I used the name once at the Mime Troupe, when I was on cleanup detail, and started a poster campaign featuring Martha Wombat, public health nurse, to remind people to take their coffee cups to the kitchen before they got moldy.

Ms. Wombat (Andrea Snow) with Mr. Sniff (Geoff Hoyle). Photo by Terry Lorant.

Besides giving you the name (or half of it), did your Mime Troupe work pre-pare you for clowning with the Pickles?

Because I had performed outdoors with the Mime Troupe for many years when I joined the Pickles, I thought: "I am a physical performer. I have a plastic face. I'll just do what I've always done, and I don't need a funny nose or oversized shoes." I was mistaken. The *commedia* stage of the Mime Troupe focused the audience's attention in a way that was not possible in the circus ring. In the ring, things needed to be more pronounced, more exaggerated, streamlined, and punctuated.

I ended up using a nose, although it wasn't a funny red one. I made my initial entrance behind a moving duck blind, which was camouflaged with leaves. Some leaves were attached to my pith helmet so that a bush appeared to separate when I popped up to scan the ring for birds. I used a gesture with binoculars to mimic bulging eyeballs when I spotted the supposed sandsniff. Peggy Snider made a fabulous dress for Ms. Wombat, which managed to be both clownish and dignified.

I wasn't aware of a tradition of women clowns that I wanted to borrow from. Of course, Joan Mankin had already clowned with the Pickles, and she is a hysterical, wonderfully funny physical actress. I am thinking more of the tradition of male clowns with enormous breasts who hit each other with their purses. This cliché I wanted to avoid.

In thinking about how to create a clown piece, I tried to understand Geoff and Larry's approach to the problem. My impulse was to come up with some kind of story, but they seemed to start with a concept or image, such as big and little. By fooling around with size and finally arriving at huge and really tiny, they ended up with a scenario.

A few years before I joined the circus, Bill and Geoff did an act I adored. Mr. Sniff was a customs official, and Willy was trying to get his suitcases through an endless inspection. To me, this was a rich situation and a funny story. But the idea for the act didn't start with the situation. Later, Geoff told me that he and Bill had as their starting point the image of a persis-tent bee buzzing around someone's head. That was it. These guys could start with a point, and the scenario would seem to radiate out, in contrast to cre-ating a linear narrative.

You performed at least one act with Bill Irwin during the 1979 season.

Bill showed up at a show on the road one time, and he managed to get into the ring, more than once probably, but this is what I remember. Geoff and Larry had some act together where at some point they stood perfectly still and stared at each other. This stare had started getting incredibly long, like a tableau. So when those guys got to the stare, Bill as Willy and Ms. Wombat went out as surveyors and measured the distance between Larry and Geoff, wrote it down on a clipboard, took a couple of other measurements, and left. Of course, Larry and Geoff had no idea this was going to happen, but they never broke the tableau. Everybody else was cracking up, the audience and especially the rest of the circus; but Geoff and Larry remained perfect statues.

You and Mr. Sniff spent some time quite close together inside a trunk.

The show opened with a trunk bit. Backstage Geoff and I were squeezed into a trunk, along with some balloons, if memory serves. Larry carried the trunk into the ring, set it down—gently, I might add—end-up, then laid it flat. He opened the lid and removed some items, like balloons. Then out came Mr. Sniff, followed by Ms. Wombat. It was clear that this wasn't a trick trunk with a false back. So what was amazing was Larry's strength and the fact that Geoff and I had fit into such a small space. Lucky for us this was the top of the show and we hadn't started sweating yet.

There was another act with the trunk where you and Geoff played violins.

That act ended with a modified "three-high." Geoff had his violin, I had mine, and Larry had his tuba. Larry sat on the end of the trunk with his feet on the ground. Geoff was on the trunk facing the opposite direction, with his behind against Larry's back and his feet on the trunk top. I climbed on top of both of them and perched with my behind against Geoff's back and my feet on Larry. Then we actually played the tune "Lady of Spain." That was the payoff.

I'm basically a clumsy person, but I just happened to take an acrobatics class a couple of years before I joined the circus. So I had a few acrobatic skills. Otherwise, I don't know if I could have stayed up there, without falling, long enough to play the tune.

Your partners had several more years of circus experience than you. Did you still feel you were "one of the clowns" that season, as you sat on their backs and played the violin?

I remember Zoe Leader [Pickle Family Circus business manager, publicist, graphic designer, juggler] telling me in 1979 that she thought the circus was more "theatrical" that year. Maybe my involvement had something to do with that. I felt I had everyone's respect and that I was invited to be a collaborator, a partner. But I deferred to Larry and Geoff, naturally. I felt that they knew what they were doing, and I wanted to learn from them.

We spent much of the season on the road, and we all camped together at the circus site. The circus felt more like a community than a company. We were a group of people into being a community, day and night. Geoff, Larry, everybody—they were all wonderful. For the period of time that we were together, the work was completely engulfing. I felt very involved. It was very much like the Mime Troupe in that regard. I felt I was a colleague of Larry and Geoff and that I was making a contribution and learning from them.

Was it different, artistically, being a clown rather than an actor?

I remember reading some "great" who said it takes nine months to perfect a role. It must take years to perfect a clown character. A character in a play has some psychological complexity, maybe some contradictions; he exists in a specific world with a set of circumstances. He's acted upon, he has to act, he changes. A clown is fixed; he *doesn't* change. There are probably exceptions to this, but it seems like clowns don't learn. They're almost elemental, like a force of nature. They enter a situation, they act and they're acted upon, and they leave essentially the same. And they're the same when they enter the next situation. Of course, a performer has years to live with his clown character, and my guess is that he or she can go very deep investigating the particular tendency or excess or essential thing his [or her] clown is.

Pino

An Interview with Diane Wasnak

D IANE WASNAK, known as Pino in the ring, joined the Pickle
Family Circus in 1989. Her first circus partner was Queenie Moon;
she subsequently became the partner of Razz, with whom she has
continued to perform over the past decade.

Wasnak has also performed the role of Puck in the Marin Shakespeare
Festival production of *A Midsummer Night's Dream.* She has appeared in
Ping Chong's performance art piece, *The Angels of Swendenborg,* in the San
Francisco–based television show *Midnight Caller,* and in a Bobby McFerrin
video. Her one-woman band was featured on the PBS television show *The
Lonesome Pine Special.* She left the Pickles in the middle of 1996, and prior
to her return in 1998, Wasnak was a clown and acrobat in the Cirque du
Soleil production of *Mystère* in Las Vegas. She received formal training from
the Antic Arts Academy at the State University of New York and learned
acrobatics from Lu Yi in San Francisco while she was a Pickle clown.

This interview was conducted in San Francisco on November 3, 1998, a few weeks before Wasnak, as Pino, performed in the winter show of the New Pickle Circus.

You studied with clowns and jugglers at the Antic Arts Academy. It sounds like a circus disguised as a school.

Our teachers were Bob Berkey [clown], Fred Garbo [juggler and clown], Michael Moschen [juggler], [and] Daniel Stein [mime]. I went there in 1982 and 1983, at the State University of New York in Purchase. We started class at eight in the morning and would go to four in the afternoon for eight weeks.

I had started taking drama classes when I was ten years old and mime classes when I was eleven. I used to perform in shows at the youth theatre program in Canton, Ohio. When I was younger than that, age five, I was allowed to watch the *Ed Sullivan Show,* and then I had to act out what I had seen for my grandparents. So I would bounce around imitating Topo Gigio, Liberace, Jack Benny, Mae West. My grandparents would say: "Stand on your head now. Sing a song, Diane." I was a born ham, and I knew I wanted to perform.

I got my first gig when I was seventeen years old. I was hired by an ice cream store in Canton to stand on the street corner in the snow in January with a big placard saying, "Come eat ice cream." I wore whiteface, snow pants, and gloves.

That's a comic act in itself—selling ice cream outdoors in winter weather.

I would say "Come in and eat some ice cream" in mime. They gave me all the ice cream I wanted to eat and ten bucks an hour, and I thought: "Hey, I can do this!" People would stop at the stoplight, and I'd run up and smash myself on their car and follow them. I was just improvising.

And that prepared you for the Pickle Family Circus?

Before the circus, I had been freelancing, doing my one-woman show and my one-woman band. I had done some storytelling and a few characters. I had a good hour and a half of material. In 1987, Tony Montanaro (a mime with whom I apprenticed in Maine) called me up and said that Judy Finelli of the Pickle Family Circus was looking for some clowns. She and I talked on the phone; we had a great conversation. Judy said she really liked my tape. It seemed like it was going to happen, but then Joan Mankin and Don Forrest came back as clowns that year. We stayed in touch, and around

October of 1988, Judy called again since Don Forrest was leaving. I had gotten frustrated playing for stupid gigs, riding my unicycle around a mall for fifty bucks. And I had a really bad party experience. I decided that if I didn't get the gig in San Francisco, I was going to quit performing and go into massage. Judy asked how soon I could start, and I said I could be on my way in two days.

Had you thought of yourself as a clown before you auditioned for the Pickles?

I certainly had done clownesque things. I don't think I labeled myself a clown. I called myself a "new vaudevillian" at that time. I still had an aversion to the Ringling Brothers "freak show clowns."

You're more comfortable with the word now?

Yeah, I'm a clown. But I use the term "physical comedian" more than "clown" because I have different characters, although they all come from my main clown character, Pino.

Pino Pompeo (Diane Wasnak). Photo by Terry Lorant.

Tell me about Pino. Where did your clown's name come from?

In 1982, when I was at the Antic Arts Academy, [the academy] was part of a big festival, Summerfare, so we could practice acts, and then we could go out and have an instant audience to try stuff out. I worked up this routine with someone named Jeff Gordon (he was a Ringling clown, but not the Jeff Gordon who was a Big Apple clown). He played a little drum while I played beer barrel polka on the accordion on his shoulders. I was dressed in a red and white striped shirt, a 1930s football helmet, weird pants, and a big black mustache.

My roommate asked, "What's your name? You've got to have a name." I had never thought about it.

I said, "I don't know."

She asked, "Well, what's your accordion's name?"

"The brand of my accordion is a Pompeo," I said.

"How about Pino Pompeo?" she asked. I liked that.

So you were named after your accordion. Do you come from a musical family?

When my grandfather was very young, he was in vaudeville. He would play accordion in between acts.

You learned accordion from him?

I learned it from my grandfather after he died. He was my big hero when I was a kid. He was a self-taught accordion player. He taught himself when he was four years old. He never read a note of music, but he could hear something once and play it. He would play along with the radio.

When my uncle was in Vietnam, we used to send tapes back and forth. My grandfather taped himself playing the accordion. After his death, I would listen to the tapes and imitate what I heard. That's how I learned to play the accordion.

So you're not a "new vaudevillian," and your accordion music is old vaudeville.

I've also always felt an affinity with the silent films of the 1920s. I like to think that Pino was transported out of a silent movie and spit out into our time. Pino is curious, bewildered, and mischievous, asking, "What's this do?" Not malicious but a prankster, a joker who likes to mess with people and things.

Pino's official dress would be very close to what Harry Langdon wore. Sideways-turned hat, a little curlicue on my head. The first year in the Pickles I wore a suit jacket that was too small and big pants. Then Pino got into spandex; it was functional—made it easier to be a mosquito in *Tossing and Turning.*

Pino doesn't speak much during her acts.

In 1985, Pino once talked through a kazoo, but I saw a few people do that and decided I was just going to be silent. Then when we were developing *Tossing and Turning,* Tandy [Beal] said, "Tell Jeff [Raz, as Razz] a bedtime story; try some gibberish." It was one of those improvisational moments that is a real turning point.

Pino tells the story of Goldilocks in gibberish. But everyone understands it, the mime is so articulate. Can you say something in Pino's language for us?

Snveneno epp ip op op bip whoop nat neet anyop. [*Editor's note:* I can't accurately transcribe the sound of the lines here. It's a cross between a drunken chipmunk and a jazz scat singer in rehearsal.]

How do you do that? Do you practice?

Practice that? No! Ever since I was little, I've done imitations. I was crazy about cartoons. I loved all the noises and all the voices. I was always playing around, making voices, although I'd never really applied it. This act was a pathway to get back to that, making noises. The way that I do the Goldilocks sketch is basically the way that I first improvised it, with the voices of the bears, the gibberish, and the big bear eating Goldilocks at the end.

There's a certain mischief or defiance in Pino's attitude; the clown speaks gibberish as if everyone should be understanding it.

It is a little defiant, but those are just my words. It's how I talk. I can understand you, and you should be able to understand Pino. I'm just trying to get a point across.

I would say that piece represents the quintessential Pino. Pino comes out with a book, reads the story, finds it a stupid story about this stupid girl who went in and ripped off the bears, and decides, "I'm going to tell this story my way!" Pino the jokester is satirizing it.

She's disrespectful?

Totally.

Actually, I don't know whether to refer to Pino as "she" or "he."

Isn't that weird? To me, Pino almost seems sexless, or very androgynous. I don't have a set gender, so that makes it easy to be a guy in a tuxedo when Razz is in a dress. Or I can be a sultry woman, or a frog.

You're a mosquito, an infant, and a pillow in Tossing and Turning, *constantly changing shapes.*

Yes. It gives me a kind of freedom. Maybe Pino has multiple personality disorders.

Puck, the character you played in A Midsummer Night's Dream, *is also a shape-changer. (At least he changes other people's shapes, or perceptions of shapes.) He flits around like a mosquito at times, too.*

Puck is pretty doggone close to Pino, though Puck is more devious and speaks a lot more, using actual words. I also did pole climbing and played the saxophone as Puck.

You've performed a number of musical acts for the Pickles, too.

Joan Mankin and I did a musical clown act that I like very much. Queenie Moon comes out to jam with the band; she has a saxophone. Then Pino comes on with an accordion. Queenie sees the accordion and says, "Get out of here; that's lame-ola."

I go get a fiddle, I play a hoedown, and she says, "No, no, get out of here." I want to play too; I like music. So I come out with a sousaphone. Queenie just looks at me and I go away. I come out with a saxophone and can't get it to start, can't get it to blow. She goes off, brings out some jumper cables, starts to play, and then I start to play. I play "Tie a Yellow Ribbon," a really cheesy song. Queenie goes, "Oh no," and pulls out her sunglasses. Then I start to play some down and dirty rhythm, and Queenie says, "Yes, okay, let's jam." We play a saxophone duet, and a gorilla—Lorenzo Pisoni—comes, and we have a little trio and do a little dance.

That act is a variation on your one-woman band.

Yes, although I haven't done the band since 1991, on *The Lonesome Pine Special.* I had put an old army trunk (that used to be my coffee table) on wheels, attacked it with a drill and saw, and put in a xylophone, a train whistle, [and] four different kinds of honking horns. Basically, I had fifteen percussive instruments on it with all the pedals on the lid when you opened it up, so I could stand on the lid and play all the drums and cymbals. Then I had an accordion with a kazoo and slide whistle attached. I could play all of them and do vocals.

One of my signature pieces was "Buffalo," an old Milton Berle vaudeville routine which I first heard when I was ten, on a record set, *Sixty Years of Laughter.* The set had all these old vaudeville sketches: Milton Berle, Mae West, Jack Benny, Smith and Dale. I still have those records, and they're really scratched up. I redid the Milton Berle sketch's music and put my own twist on it. I've been thinking of putting my band back together, but it was a nightmare to travel with it.

Some artists have trouble traveling with other musicians; you have trouble traveling with your one-person band. But you enjoy working with other clowns, too?

I think I can say the same for both Queenie and Razz. I love them dearly, but as Pino I just want to irritate the hell out of them. [Loud laughter follows.]

How do you irritate them?

Jeff's so big . . . I go behind his back, and when he turns I keep behind him—crawl under his legs, then come up behind him, go "Bah!" and scare him.

You have crawled all over him. You also dance with him.

Where I'm dressed in the tux? That's our drag number.

Even for drag it's unusual; he's much bigger than you.

Oh yeah. He is big. I'm "Pino Suavo." It's a ballroom dance. I have to climb up a little ladder to reach him. He walks over me. We try to be very serious, beautiful, and debonair.

If you're not, at least you're very funny trying. You've also played the role of a baby with Queenie and with Razz.

Yes. Electra, the demon baby from hell. That was the first routine Joan and I worked on when I joined the circus; it was her idea.

Later you became the leaping baby, jumping off the teeterboard, and Razz had to catch you.

When I first joined the circus, I didn't do acrobatics. I knew how to walk wire and ride a unicycle. I was just hired to be funny in that first year, 1989. The next year, Lu Yi came. I started learning acrobatics when I was twenty-eight. I did pole climbing, hoop diving, and teeterboard for the first time in 1990 in *[La La] Luna Sea,* following five and a half months of training with Lu Yi.

You've been with the Pickles for close to a decade; what's changed?

When I first joined, the shows were in the open air. We had bleacher trucks, and I drove one of the trucks. I lived in the back of my truck, or in a tent, camping out. I liked it.

There was a big change in the amount of equipment when we did *Luna Sea* in 1990; it got really big and heavy, and the cast got smaller. Everybody was in everything. I was doing teeterboard, pole climbing, hoop diving, playing music, doing word stuff. I was on the rigging crew. I was onstage the entire time except for intermission, in a two-hour show twice a day, sometimes outside in 100-plus degree weather. I couldn't do that now.

It wasn't as much work when *Luna Sea* was performed indoors. Outside we had to pound stakes, put up bleachers, pad them, hang the rigging bats, hang the sidewall. The show outdoors was killing us. The Conservation Corps used to help us set up, which was a godsend.

I remember being in Bend, Oregon, one summer at night, with a full moon, under a blanket of stars. The lights on the stage were regular floodlights, and it was beautiful. I was able to make eye contact with everyone in the audience. Some of the open-air nighttime shows of *Luna Sea* were pure magic.

The nature of the performance changes when you move indoors.

Indoors, you're performing for a different audience—an audience that is used to going to the theatre. I like having everybody. Many different kinds of people come in for a circus; it's eight bucks, and they get popcorn, as opposed to "circus in a theatre" where people think, "We have to dress up now."

As a performer you sense the difference.

Definitely. The audience is definitely more restrained in a theatre. I remember a very fancy theatre in Connecticut, with people coming in dressed in black. During the preshow I was messing with people, trying to break them up. It was a challenge. There were some people giving me some looks, and I'd give them their looks right back.

You're leaving a role in the Las Vegas Cirque du Soleil to return to the New Pickle Circus this winter. There are some differences between these two circuses.

I see a lot of differences. The most obvious difference is money. The first time I saw Cirque du Soleil was in Montreal in 1987. I paid eight bucks, sat in the front row, and it was the most wonderful show I've ever seen in my life. I told myself, "I want to do this." That was before I received any calls from the Pickles.

I had grown up in the Midwest and associated circus with Shriners, three rings, sitting way up in the balcony, eating popcorn, and seeing weird things. But I was touched by the first Cirque du Soleil. I've seen every show that they've done. It's technically amazing.

When I saw them in 1988, I felt, "Hey, this isn't like the first time that I saw them." Each year it has gotten slicker and slicker to the point where it's cookie-cutter. They have a formula. Most of the performers in an ongoing show are gymnasts; they train to do circus acts, and then they put a mask on. Cirque tells them, "Watch this video, and do the movement just like this."

They called me up and said, "We understand you do a baby character." I said, "Yes, I've done a baby character for about ten years." "We have an opening here," they told me; "we have this character and it's always changing and evolving." So I packed up my truck, put in all my musical instruments, my bike. Then they sent me two videos. Neither video showed that there were two babies in the show, although I heard there were two. The baby in the video threw a great big red ball in the audience, and I thought, "Well, that's interesting."

You had done that yourself?

Ten years earlier. The Pickle Family Circus had performed in Stony Brook and got a highly favorable review in the *New York Times*. I know that a lot of people from Cirque du Soleil came to see that show, with the baby and the red ball.

You could consider it a great compliment, if they liked your act so much that they added it to their repertoire. But it seems Cirque du Soleil does not always encourage its artists to be original or create new acts.

I had planned to change the character of the baby I saw on the video. I told them, "My baby's got an edge." As soon as I got there, they wanted me to make my hair blonde and grow it long so they could make ponytails. I thought they were joking and found out they're weren't. Then I found out there was another baby in the show, and I wondered, "Where do I fit into this?" In terms of my role in the show, I'm kind of a walking set piece, except when the big baby's sick. There was huge miscommunication. I was also given orders not to look at the audience, not to have any contact with the audience.

It sounds like a preset show, not what you'd expect in a circus, particularly not from clowns. It is different clowning for the Pickles?

With the Pickles, I can be myself. I'm given the opportunity to be creative and to be who I am. My year-and-a-half incarceration with Cirque du Soleil taught me that there are things more important than money: one is to follow your heart, and do what you love. So I'm going to do more writing, more acting, voice-overs, tour my own show in the future.

The Pickles were definitely a big part of my life. I don't know if they will be a big part of my life again, but it's a wonderful place to come back to. I found my niche with them. I was able to write my own material with a partner, [was] able to say: "Hey, let's have a strong man and a monkey climb a pole!" and have my opinion matter. It was my family; it is my family.

Saxophones

A Clown Act by Joan Mankin and Diane Wasnak

QUEENIE MOON—*Joan Mankin—is revealed by a spotlight. She wears gold lamé pants, a silver jacket with a white flower pattern, red boots, and her own wild red hair, and she carries a saxophone on a cord around her neck. Music with a jazz beat comes from the band. She dances over to the microphone, picks up the mike, and speaks. Harvey Robb, a saxophonist, and Helena Jack, trumpet and keyboard player, both members of the Pickle Family Circus Band, answer her from their seats, onstage with the rest of the band.*

> *Queenie Moon:* Hey there, what's happen-ning, duds?
> *Harvey Robb:* Ah, Queenie, the concept is not duds, it's dudes, so get with it.
> *Queenie Moon:* Truly, truly, I said now, what's happen-ning, dudes?
> *Harvey Robb:* That's more like it.

Helena Jack: Now listen up, girlfriend. Yes, baby, you all know what I'm getting ready to say, don't you? There's only four dudes in this band. There's a woman here, and all you women know we need to get our recognition, anytime. You should be ashamed of yourself. Don't you all agree with me? Okay dear, let's get it out now.

Queenie Moon: Truly, truly. What's happen-ning, dudes and dude-dess?

Harvey Robb: All right, Queenie, that's it.

Queenie Moon: Now what do you say, let us preserve.

Harvey Robb: Ah, Queenie, could you possibly mean: "Let's jam"?

Queenie Moon: Truly, truly. What is it, Harvey?

Harvey Robb: What it is, Queenie.

(Music starts, Queenie struts to center as bass plays rhythm. She dances, bends forward low, and then blows saxophone while bending over backwards. Sound is cool jazz, and she raises her arm in triumph.

Pino—Diane Wasnak—enters, dressed in white shirt, black jacket, black pants, and black derby hat. [She looks far from hip.] She holds an accordion and tentatively shuffles closer to Queenie. Pino tries to play "Tie a Yellow Ribbon." She surprises and scares Queenie, who lifts up her sunglasses to peer at Pino. Queenie then makes a gesture of "square" with her hands and sends Pino off.

Queenie snaps her fingers and the audience claps its hands as the band plays a cool rhythm. She speaks to audience while it is clapping rhythm.)

Queenie: All right now, everybody stick out your tongue. Oooh, that's nasty!

(Pino returns with a violin and tries to join in with square dance music. Queenie's knees start knocking in shock. She takes away Pino's violin bow, and Pino scrapes the violin against the bow in an effort to keep playing. Queenie draws "square" again in the air, and Pino exits.

Pino very quickly returns with a sousaphone but exits as soon as Queenie stares at her with disapproval. Offstage, Pino plays one low sousaphone note, and Queenie checks behind her to see who farted.

Queenie starts to blow a long note on the sax and lies on her back on the floor while playing. Pino returns with a saxophone, and Queenie now welcomes her with "Let us exhale!" *The two of them try to play together, but no sound comes out of Pino's instrument. Queenie gets a jumper cable and jump-starts Pino's sax from her own, so both instruments work.*

At first Pino plays a tune Queenie considers square. Then Queenie puts some sunglasses on Pino [both of them wear pairs] and says, "All right sister, let's jam!" *After some difficulty getting together, they begin to play a sax duet. Pino bumps Queenie with sax at one point. Finally, they're playing jazz together when a large gorilla [Lorenzo Pisoni in gorilla suit] enters wearing sunglasses and white tennis shoes and plays his sax. Queenie and Pino stop, glare, then all three play same tune as a saxophone trio. They dance around the stage and off.)*

Razz

An Interview with Jeff Raz

JEFF RAZ joined the Pickle Family Circus during its 1991 season. Known as Razz in the ring, he has continued to perform clown acts with his partner, Pino, in the circus and elsewhere. Prior to his years with the Pickles, he juggled with the Bay City Reds and performed as a clown and juggler for Make-a-Circus, the San Francisco New Vaudeville Festival, and the J. P. Booker Early American Circus. He was cofounder of the group Vaudeville Nouveau and acted with it as well as with the Dell'Arte Players. Raz has also appeared in the Flying Karamazov Brothers' production of Shakespeare's *A Comedy of Errors*, directed by Robert Woodruff for Lincoln Center and PBS television, and played the role of Bottom in Shakespeare's *A Midsummer Night's Dream*, with Pino as Puck, in the Marin Shakespeare Festival. He is the author of numerous plays and one-person performance pieces, including *Father-Land, The Great Big Rainbow Tent, Noah's Floating House Party*, and, most recently, *Birthmark*. He has taught circus skills and theatre at the Dell'Arte School, Ringling Bros. Clown College, the University of Nebraska, and the San Francisco School for the Arts.

This interview was conducted in San Francisco on October 8, 1998, not long after Raz agreed to perform with his partner, Diane Wasnak, in the 1998 New Pickle Circus season.

You saw the Pickles in their early years, didn't you?

Yes, almost from the beginning.

You were more enthusiastic about some Pickle Family Circus seasons than others.

Although I knew and liked most of the performers, I didn't particularly like the Pickles' aesthetic in the early days.

How early?

Before I joined. *[Laughter.]* Seriously, up until the late '80s, it was an act-to-act circus, and I would enjoy certain acts. I loved *The Three Musicians,* I always loved Bill's stuff and usually loved Geoff's stuff. I was once a student of Larry's, and we had an often contentious relationship; when I could get past that, I would usually love his stuff, too. But I would sometimes get bored with the act-to-act, old circus feel of the Pickle shows.

Not all of the acts were that good. I was interested in the dance elements and with their attempts to tell stories, either with the clowning or with a whole scene *[Café des Artistes]*. But I often didn't feel that the show worked as a whole. Remember, this is coming from the point of view of a young performer trying to find his way in the circus world.

Before you joined the Pickles, you were a juggler, and it seems that juggling led you toward clowning in the circus.

Yes, that's true. I learned to juggle when I was fourteen at the Renaissance Fair. In 1978 I joined the Bay City Reds, juggling with Billy Kessler, Merle Goldstone, and Wendy Parkman. Before that, I had a leather goods business on Telegraph Avenue in Berkeley. I closed down my business and moved to San Francisco the day I heard that I had the job with the Reds. I made fifty dollars a week with the Bay City Reds, which was riches compared to what I had been living on.

Billy, Merle, and I started the act with a comedy nine-club juggling routine, which would hold up as a hot act to this day. We'd fake a drop and Wendy would come out of the audience, pick up the dropped club, and get caught in the middle of the juggling pattern. We did a clown act a few times, and Wendy, Bill, and I did an acrobatics act that we learned from the owner of Dance Your Ass Off disco, Stu Goldberg.

By '78, I had been clowning already in the J. P. Booker Early American Circus. My friend Mark Sackett, who became my partner in Vaudeville Nouveau, got me a job there. I worked for them on and off for a year, and I was the boss clown. I was also the only clown. Later I worked with my long-time friend Janet Goulston. I did an animal act with a pony, some juggling, and some other shtick. Mark and I worked on a rope-walking act; we both walked on the same slack rope and passed the juggling clubs. We did it once in a show, didn't drop, and decided not to push our luck—we never performed it again.

You also took some classes or workshops in circus skills.

Yes, in Joe Bellan's Studio on Bush Street there was a school called CTC, Cultural Training Center, in the mid-'70s. Larry Pisoni was teaching a circus skills class, Bill Irwin was teaching a clowning class, [and] Richard Seyd was teaching, too, I think. It never occurred to me to take Bill's class; I was too macho for clowning. I've always regretted that. I did get a great foundation in circus skills from Larry's class: rolling globe, slack rope, stilts, rolla bolla, acrobatics. I learned to stand on Larry's shoulders. Geoff Hoyle learned to stand on mine, as I recall. Wendy Parkman and other future Pickles were in the same class, along with members of Everybody's Family Circus, which I worked with for a couple of years. I was the worst acrobat in the class and the best juggler. Since we always ended with juggling, my ego was left intact enough to come to the next class.

In 1979, after a year with the Reds, I went to study and teach at the Dell'Arte School. I was twenty years old. I couldn't afford the school, so I made a deal with them: I taught juggling for five weeks, and they gave me free tuition for ten weeks.

I was up there in Blue Lake at the Dell'Arte School when the Pickle Family Circus held auditions in San Francisco. Billy, Wendy, and I decided to audition with our acrobatic act. I couldn't make it down for the audition, but since Larry had seen all three of us, I figured it would work out. He hired Billy and Wendy and not me. They became Pickle stars. Billy made his name in the trampoline act, and Wendy of course did trapeze, among other things. So that broke up our threesome. I was pissed off. Since then, I've actually been quite thankful about the way it turned out. I loved working with Billy and Wendy, but if I had joined the Pickles in '79, I wouldn't have been able to get into the experimentation I did with the Dell'Arte Players and then Vaudeville Nouveau.

In Vaudeville Nouveau you were still juggling?

Yes. Mark Sackett and I started a duet in 1982, after we both found ourselves out of work. We were doing juggling and music. He's a professional musician. In our signature act, he played a flute and I juggled silver balls choreographed to the music. Dan Mankin made it a trio in '83. As we developed Vaudeville Nouveau, we used all of our circus and music skills, but it became very character-based. We were very interested in telling stories and creating strong characters while we were juggling and doing acrobatics.

What kind of characters did you portray?

I was the Number Three. Danny Mankin was the Number One; Mark was the Number Two. Danny would be the leader, relating to the audience. Mark was the dumb one, like Paul Fratellini. I was the Albert Fratellini, the wild card. I would yell things out. My pants would fall down. I would come in screaming with a rubber chicken. When someone needed to turn into a full-size chicken, my clothes would rip away, and I had the chicken costume on.

So you portrayed a giant chicken?

Yes, in *Savage Chicken.* The play was a whole evening, not just an act, and it was Vaudeville Nouveau's hit in 1985. We took it to Europe. Jael Weisman directed. He also directed the Bay City Reds, the Dell'Arte Players, and much of my recent work.

Savage Chicken was about the chicken gods. The premise was, if there are gods for every creature, then the chicken gods might decide to make an example of us for our mistreatment of rubber chickens (rubber chickens were our favorite prop). We had masks made for these chicken gods and a little puppet stage with puppets of us.

The chicken gods kept torturing us as we kept torturing chickens. At one point we had a four-foot-tall chicken puppet, and we did a doctor's act, where we cut open the chicken. I had the worst line there. I came in with a potted plant and started hooking it up to the chicken's wing. Danny asked me, "Big Guy, what are you doing?" I replied, "I'm connecting the ivy." I loved what would happen next. It would start with a laugh and slowly evolve into a full "BOOO" as I stood and milked it. It was great fun. In the end, the chicken gods turned me into a chicken, I'd rip away to this chicken outfit, and we would do a nine club/one rubber chicken juggling routine.

We did five or six plays. *Aesthetic Peril* (in two versions), *Lost Art, The Detective,* which Joe Chaikin (of the Open Theatre) directed. *Savage Chicken* was the one people liked best. The second version of *Aesthetic Peril* also played very well. I left the group in '89. Dan and Mark kept Vaudeville Nouveau going into the early '90s.

You developed plays—at least narrative forms—that incorporated circus arts in Vaudeville Nouveau.

Yes. The Pickles tried it too, with *Café des Artistes,* which I didn't think was a great act, although I enjoyed it. The circus skills weakened the plot, and the plot weakened the circus skills. I found it entertaining, though more for the circus skills than the story.

I have to say that at the same time, Bill Irwin was performing *The Regard of Flight,* which was great. Bill really set a standard for integrating circus skills and theatre.

Some of the things we did in *The Comedy of Errors* worked well, with the Flying Karamazov Brothers, Avner the Eccentric, Wendy Parkman, and some other Pickle performers.

You performed Shakespeare with the Karamazov Brothers? The jugglers, not the characters from Dostoyevsky?

In '82, Mark and I were hired as utility players. Each of us could play an instrument. He was a professional flute player; I could fake a few instruments. We both juggled and did acrobatics and were actors to some degree. I ended up playing seven roles; so did Mark. We did everything. We were the utility guys.

That first run of *Comedy of Errors,* at the Goodman Theater in Chicago, made me very frustrated. Mark and I had been asking where you find scripts for our kind of work. I had been thinking that Shakespeare was a kindred spirit—some of his work came out of *commedia.* Then we got into rehearsals and found that the Karamazovs were thinking, "This Shakespeare stuff doesn't make sense." It seemed that they just wanted to get to their shtick as quickly as possible. It made me crazy. Here Mark and I were, people who could handle the lines (at least in our minds we could handle them), with almost no lines; and there were the Karamazovs, who by their own admission weren't interested in Shakespeare and had tons of them. The approach, which was "shtick it until you can't recognize the text," really bothered me.

Luckily, Robert Woodruff, the director, didn't listen to my complaints. He knew that he had a group of very funny people. He said: "It's going to be a great show, but it has to be on its own terms. That's what I'm directing. The text is less funny than these people. This group of people really trying to do this text is death. We'll use the text when it works (with people like Sophie Schwab, who was an actress who played Adriana)."

By the time we took the show to Broadway in '87, I had figured out what we were doing. I remember a point in rehearsal when Paul Magid, one of the Karamazovs, had a long monologue. Woodruff placed Vaudeville Nouveau [Mark and I] upstage and had us do our entire acrobatics act during Paul's speech. Woodruff stopped us, saying he wasn't hearing anything and that there was some information in the monologue that the audience had to have. So he told us to do some acrobatics but keep it all low, on the ground. He stopped us again, saying: "It's still too much. I just want you guys to enter and stretch." Sackett and I sat on the floor and stretched. But we worked out a bit where we quietly tried to one-up each other with our stretching, and we would have our whole side of the audience watching us instead of listening to Paul's monologue. But Paul was no sap; he had ample opportunity to get his licks in.

I have to give the Karamazovs credit here—they were very funny and the show was very successful. We had a six-piece band, the Kamikaze Ground Crew, playing the show. The Karamazovs and Vaudeville Nouveau were very interested in juggling to music and had gotten very advanced at it in different ways. So there was a formal musical structure to the production with a lot of innovative juggling. And Shakespeare's text was formal. Then there were these wild people, and Woodruff was good enough to turn them loose. By the third time we did the production, at Lincoln Center, after the Goodman Theatre and the Olympic Arts Festival in L.A., we had genuine friendships, genuine chemistry, and we were a finely tuned ensemble.

You also performed A Midsummer Night's Dream *for the Marin Shakespeare Festival; but that was a different experience.*

Yes, the producers asked me to play Bottom, and I asked them to bring Diane [Wasnak] in as Puck. Diane and I were already a team with the Pickles, and we wanted to work in another setting. We brought our circus sensibility to Shakespeare rather than the other way around. In this case, though, we were imposing our circus sensibility on a group of actors—many who had no "physical theater" background. For example, I basically directed the Pyramus and Thisbe scene. Everyone was game, and the show worked well.

For Puck, Diane had a pole built into the set; she would climb it and jump all over the place. When Puck puts the ass's head on Bottom, Diane jumped on my shoulders, and we did an acrobatic cross together. Bottom is always a clown role. Puck is not often, but the way Diane played the role, it really came alive. As Bottom, I entered through the audience and played it throughout with a New Vaudeville intimacy. We were outside, like Shakespeare's actors, and I played with the audience as I imagine they did. The skills and the tricks were interesting, and they fit Shakespeare.

From a circus standpoint, I concentrated on Pyramus and Thisbe. For Thisbe's speech over the dead Pyramus, we did a "dead and alive" routine, an old clown routine. For the ending, we did a "rustic" juggling act with Puck joining in for some acrobatics.

Shakespeare offers a comic nightmare with Bottom's dream. You dealt with another aspect of sleep—insomnia—in the Pickles production of Tossing and Turning.

It's my second year with the Pickles, 1992. Here comes the new director, Tandy Beal, a dancer, with the idea to do a play about the moment when you can't sleep, about insomnia. Diane and I didn't know each other well— we had only worked together for a year—but we both knew that this was wrong. A whole show about sleep? The audience will nap until intermission and then go home.

It turned out to be brilliant. It was not about dreaming, not about sleep, but the weird space in between. Tandy's an insomniac and had created a solo piece on the theme, so she knew the subject was rich.

Tandy had seen my solo show, *Father-Land*, and she said, "You did a bunch of characters in that; now why don't you try a goodnight fairy tale in gibberish?" I did one in rehearsal, just for Tandy and Diane, and it bombed. So she asked Diane to try "Goldilocks and the Three Bears." She didn't want to, but Tandy pushed and Diane did it brilliantly; the story you see onstage is basically the one she improvised that day in rehearsal. I was a bit jealous, but I knew she had a gem. I've watched that piece hundreds of times in the last seven years.

When we were trolling for ideas, I said I loved that Peking opera "fight in the dark," and it led to Diane becoming a mosquito. We gave our acrobatic trainer, Lu Yi, the reference to the Peking opera fight in the dark, and he helped us work out the acrobatics. I play the straight man, who wakes up with a mosquito in his bedroom and does everything he can to kill the mosquito. He starts swatting it with a pillow, but it escapes and climbs up on his shoulders. We pace out like we are having a duel. I see her and do a shooting ducks in a gallery bit to hit the mosquito behind the bed stand. "Ting, ting, ting." Finally, I try a huge flyswatter, which breaks over her head. In the end, I spray it with insecticide, which the mosquito likes because it's a mutant. On the blackout, it's cutting me up with a giant knife and fork and sucking my blood with a straw. The mosquito act did not have music, only sound effects, but it was very carefully worked out with the band.

For the opening number, Tandy asked, "What if you did an act where Diane never touched the ground?" It's a very dancerly concept. So we threw that idea to Lu Yi, and his eyes lit up, because he saw it as an acrobatic concept. The outcome was that while I'm up there as ringmaster delivering this greeting to the audience, I'm either pretending not to notice, or not noticing, that Pino is all over me, doing every acrobatic move that she can do without touching the ground.

My costume was a nightshirt/tuxedo. The bed was a consistent prop. My acts would start in the bed. A juggling act started as I got rolled out of the bed. Diane's "Three Bears" started with different members of the company—Russian, French Canadian, Chinese—reading me the story in different languages. I sat in the bed and watched.

Pino had a consistent character, too. She was the pest. I was the narrator and the pestered. It fit well with our sizes, too.

As your partnership with Pino progressed, you consciously based some of the acts on the fact that you are much larger than she is?

Yes, especially the acrobatic acts, as in act 2 of *Tossing and Turning*, when she was a pillow. She's got this costume that literally makes her into a pillow. The act starts with the company members doing a sort of restless sleeping dance with pillows. Then Diane and I are there, and I'm asleep on her, wrestling with the pillow. It was hard acrobatically. She jumps and sits on my feet and we do a Risley act [a foot-juggling act using people as juggled "objects"], which is hard enough without the pillow. Then I have to turn, and she's lying across my feet, rolls down my feet, and over my head. The pillow helped with this—it saved us from some bruises. There was music which we had to follow for the whole act.

You concluded the show by stepping into a woman's dress, as if in some strange dream, with Pino in a baby carriage. How did you get into a dress?

It wasn't the first time; I did a drag number in Vaudeville Nouveau. In the Pickles, it was for the first act closer, the teeterboard act. Diane had a great character which we hadn't used, a baby. So Tandy had the idea to use the teeterboard act for this bouncing baby. The macho-ness of the teeterboard played against the baby. The act was called "Teetertots." I was the main catcher in the act, so I played the mother. I enter sleepwalking [and] step behind this giant red ball—slats of elastic material—change rapidly, and step right out in a housedress. Diane comes out as the baby with this giant bottle; we do a bit of shtick. Then the rest of the company comes screaming onstage and we do the act. A mother and her septuplets.

You didn't speak much during Tossing and Turning.

No, only in the opening, as the ringmaster. I said more in *Jump Cuts!* You know, Diane doesn't speak at all as Pino (she does her Goldilocks story in gibberish). Pino and Razz don't have much verbal dialogue. But we did have physical dialogue.

"Physical dialogue"? I haven't heard that term before.

Maybe I invented it. "Copyright 1998." It's verbal dialogue done physically. If I did coin a new phrase there, it's not a new idea. Bill Irwin (or the publicist for his show) has been pushing that idea for *Fool Moon:* it's a play without words but with themes, motifs, everything that's in a play except for words.

I think Tossing and Turning *also had that—if not a story, then a series of thematically related acts. Were you pleased with that structure for the show?*

I loved it. After years of looking to narrative theatre for a structural model, I would say that the structure of dance or dance theatre worked much better, because dancers have physical dialogue. Look at the choreography of Joe Goode or Kimi Okada. The theme for *Tossing and Turning* was strong and flexible; we inserted a lot of acts into it over the course of two years. And it put the clowns in the wonderful position of being the storytellers, being the connective tissue.

That also happened in the next New Pickle Circus production, Jump Cuts!

Yes. I felt that the theme for *Jump Cuts!* was less flexible, a little more brittle. It's about two innocents caught in the fantasy of the movies. It felt stronger at the top, with a lot of quick images which resonated.

The opening Wild West shoot-out was almost a ballet. But the clown acts were not as surreal as the ones in Tossing and Turning. *Maybe they were too focused on evoking film images.*

Maybe. It's always hard to second-guess the creative process. Our best clown act, the one that we still do, was the dance in the Romance section of *Jump Cuts!* (The other sections were the Western, Film Noir, and the Bizarre.) I was in this giant pink, fluffy dress, Diane was in a little silver tux, and we danced. A little tango, different moves. At one point she falls down and I walk right over her. Maybe it had a little of Fred Astaire, but it was more edgy than that.

It's an act of role reversal.

Yes. We open with our backs to the audience. We get the laugh, because I've got this strapless on. She's a real debonair little fellow. I take out a hand-kerchief, drop it, and she does some shtick retrieving it. I notice that she's too short for me, and I flirt with someone in the audience. Then she jumps up on my leg and kisses my hand—I'm smitten. We have a couple of tango moves. She comes up to my sternum, a little short. She dips me, which is a nice move. I pull myself up on her. (She can pick me up; she's very strong.)

Then I walk over her and realize that she's looking up my dress, so I do a little take there. She's licking her lips. Then at the end she brings out a step-

Razz (Jeff Raz, *left*) and partner Pino (Diane Wasnak) dance in *Let's Face the Music and . . .* Photo by David Allen. Courtesy Friends of Olympia Station/New Pickle Circus.

ladder [and] finally gets up to my height. I have a rose behind my ear, and we end posed with the rose.

That's dance, character acting, and clowning all together in one act—quite an impressive combination. There's some stylistic continuity from the first Pickle shows, with their dances, to your dance in Jump Cuts!

And the band continues to play, live, always an important part of the Pickles.

Juggling in the Pickles also approaches dance at times, as the jugglers move to music.

Yes, absolutely. I'm proud of the work I've done juggling with music and tried to do something new every year with the Pickles. When I introduce a juggling act I do with Bach music, especially when I introduce it to kids, I often say, "The balls are going to dance to the music."

Music, live music, is key to the Pickles. Before every show we did in my years with the Pickles, the band would play while the performers warmed up. Often, I would juggle to the music to get loose. Bill Belasco, the drummer, would invariably pick up on what I was doing, and we'd play off each other. After the band finished, Diane would always go to the drum kit and say: "What time is it? It's polka time." Then she played beer barrel polka on the drum. It would drive me crazy, and everyone loved it. There was a link between the music and the inspiration it created, even before the show started.

Earlier you started to say something about the Pickle Family Circus being clown-centered; is that unusual from your perspective?

It certainly isn't late-twentieth-century American circus tradition. In Ringling and other "traditional" circuses, the clowns were at the bottom of the corporate ladder, right below tiger piss. I'll give you an example: My partner Janet Goulston and I did a clown trainer and dancing bear act in the Booker circus. It was put in a slot to cover the tiger cage coming down. The act couldn't have any structure; it had to last as long as it took the roustabouts to take the cage down. If they were slow, we had to keep going, well past where we should have ended. If they were fast, we were cut off in the middle of the act. The rule for clowns is, when the ringmaster blows the whistle, you exit. Basically, there can be no beginning, middle, or end to a clown act.

The Pickles had no tiger cages, of course. If we ever had a tiger cage, it would have had to wait for the clowns to finish their act. The show is about humanity, its greatest feats and its greatest folly. The clowns worked with the director to shape a seamless show. It is not about who gets hurt or about getting from one act to another. The clowns got to create their acts and to finish them without any help from the tigers. What more could I ask for?

Let's Face the Music and . . .

A Clown Act by Jeff Raz and Diane Wasnak

T HE ACT *begins with six men in white tuxedos and top hats dancing with six half-built female mannequins wearing red dresses and boas. They dance in front of a large two-dimensional cutout of a heart, colored red, with a decorative blue border. At first, the dance is sedate ballroom movement. As it progresses, the men begin to swing more wildly with their partners and throw them into the air. It looks like the women (mannequins) are doing flips into the air, fantastic turns, and they land in the arms of their partners. The couples conclude their dance. Blackout.*

Lights up on the large red heart, which splits in two to reveal two figures with their backs to the audience. Razz and Pino stand next to each other. We see the back of his dress, the back of her tux. They turn around and face the audience. We see a large man (Razz) in a strapless pink ballroom gown with fluffy pink feathers on the neckline. He is smiling coyly. We also see a small woman (Pino) in a silver tuxedo and silver porkpie hat.

The four-piece Pickle band plays the tango "String Theory" by musical director Jeffrey Gaeto as Raz takes out a gauzy pink handkerchief, waves it toward Pino, and drops it. She retrieves it eagerly.

They begin to dance. Their differences in height and weight make it hard for them to dance together comfortably. Razz dismisses Pino and walks off to flirt with the audience. With a snappy look, Pino gets his attention and runs up his left thigh and locks her right leg behind his neck. Her head is above his. Razz offers his hand for a kiss. Pino waves her tongue out for a lewd smooch. She dismounts and they both take a few deep breaths.

The tango now begins in earnest, with Pino dipping Razz. Surprisingly, he doesn't fall, and as she lifts him back to his feet, the dance moves across the floor. A moment later, Pino slips under Razz, who continues dancing right over her while she is on her back on the floor. Once his wide dress has passed across her, she is not flattened but invigorated by the sights seen under the petticoats. She sits up, smiles, and licks her lips.

The tango heats up. After Pino spins Razz, she finds herself nearly engulfed by Razz's ample, pink-feathered bosom. He extracts her, only to find that his scarf is now in her mouth.

Pino runs off and trades the scarf for a short red stepladder. She returns, runs toward Razz with it, and climbs up the ladder so she's now his height. After a few near misses, they find themselves in an embrace, cheek to cheek. The two clowns, one standing on a stepladder, hold their romantic pose and smile with a rose between them. Blackout.

Tandy Beal

An Interview

T ANDY BEAL served as artistic director of the New Pickle Circus from 1993 to 2000. Circus presentations she directed include *Tossing and Turning* (1992), *Jump Cuts!* (1994), *Jingle Pickles* (1996), *The Big Bang . . . and Other Rude Noises!* (1997), *Step Right Up!* (1998), *Circus of Song* (2000), and *Eyes Wide Open* (a duet show with the clowns Pino and Razz, toured at irregular intervals). She is a performer and director/choreographer and has performed as a solo artist and with her own ensemble around the world. As a choreographer, Beal has created and performed more than one hundred dance and theatre works since 1974, when she began her dance company.

Her career includes creating a work for NASA's Search for Extra-Terrestrial Intelligence Project with Carl Sagan and Frank Drake; a United States Information Agency–sponsored tour of Eastern Europe; acting off-Broadway; guest performances in the United States with the Atlanta Ballet, Momix, and Remy Charlip and in Europe with Caroline Carlson; touring for several years with the Nikolais Dance Theatre; staging opera,

This interview was conducted in San Francisco on November 18, 1998, prior to the opening of *Step Right Up!*

including Bobby McFerrin's opera conducting debut; writing, directing, and choreographing a Japanese production of the Moscow Circus; and a variety of projects with composers Lou Harrison, Jon Scoville, Frank Zappa, and John Adams. Film and television credits include an Emmy-award-winning PBS special with Bobby McFerrin; choreography for Tim Burton's *The Nightmare Before Christmas;* segments for the TV series *Everyday Spirituality* by Thomas Moore and MTV's *The Garden;* staging Voicestra for the *Today* show and *Arsenio Hall Show;* writing and directing *Figure of Speech on Hildegard von Bingen* for the American Film Institute; and dance and theatre works shown on the national TV stations of Japan, Hong Kong, and Switzerland.

A number of the Pickle clowns have created comic dances, drawing on the eccentric dance tradition and parodying Hollywood spectacle. I'm intrigued that circus clowns would also be comic dancers.

If you take an artist like Jacques Tati, you can't call him just a clown or a dancer or an actor; he's walking in all those worlds. The connection between them has to do with timing. Dancers are trained in time, to know when the moment is right. A clown has to find the right moment, too; the joke doesn't happen unless the timing is perfect.

Also, it's very natural that when you're working in a realm that is physical and nonverbal, you're going to rely on the craft that is inherent in the process of choreography.

Your own interest in the arts clearly extends beyond dance and dance choreography into circus, opera, theatre.

I'm interested in the challenge of how to fit the content to the right form. My training was in dance, but my home has always been theatre. Dance taught me the craft of shaping time, space, and motion, and this craft translates well to other disciplines. But dance alone has never been the only reason to make a show. I've always colored outside of the lines, using whatever tools were necessary to make the work strongest, whether it was trapeze in a work about William Blake or dance in a circus. Sometimes it is dance, sometimes language, sometimes circus, sometimes film that is the right choice.

Communicating an idea or a feeling has always been the important thing for me. I have never understood when a choreographer says she/he doesn't care whether the audience "gets" it or not. Perhaps because I grew up with two Broadway actors, I saw very early that we only had food on the table when the show communicated well to an audience.

You've communicated through a narrative or story line in some of your dance and circus presentations.

When we started to create *Tossing and Turning,* I envisioned Jeff Raz as Everyman. I saw him as the innocent with this daily event we all go through: going to sleep. When I conceived Diane Wasnak's character, she had a dual role—as the Sandman, who could bring us into the world of dreams, and as the mischief maker who keeps us from sleeping.

The evening offered a series of beautiful images and actions, unified by Razz's insomnia. Did you begin with several images in mind?

I began *Tossing and Turning* with the subject of insomnia. I had already done a solo dance/theatre show, *Night Life,* on that theme. I had done so much research on it for my solo show that I had many ideas left. I couldn't use them all in the solo, because it was just a single person onstage.

So I had tons of images when I walked in for *Tossing and Turning:* the sheep tumbling over the bed, the Olympics score cards going up, climbing the poles to the stars, the gibberish fairy tale that Diane did so brilliantly. The central image was a man trying to sleep. The dreams were the acts, and the clowning was usually the insomnia. I saw Jeff practicing with spoons, and that developed into the "food parade." It turned into the short eccentric dance of the tomato sandwich, the pickle, and the piece of cheese. The big cheese! *[Laughter.]*

It was a very funny, surreal parade across the stage.

I also remember having the image of Queen of the Night passing through, leaving behind her eight sleeping people hugging pillows. They all sat together, showing big "Z"s under the pillows as they turned over. The show was rich with metaphors. I think that our lives get revealed in metaphors. The metaphors onstage allow you to jump into your own personal Rorschach test and discover yourself as well as the work that's in front of you. For me, the metaphor is always a rich source. Because it's image or metaphor, not strict narrative, it allows you to surf through a wide variety of your own experiences.

As a result, the work is poetic as well as comic. Do you think you could have created that sort of comedy and dance elsewhere, outside the circus?

I think I've always created works that mingled dance and humor. However, working in the circus allows me to be so much broader than what the dance world prefers. Similarly, I adored working on movement for characters in the film *The Nightmare Before Christmas,* because I would have scenes done two or three different ways with each piece of music and then improvise it as well; and the director always loved the craziest version that I did! Here was someone going, "Yeah, get crazier." The circus is that way, too. But in the dance world, because there are issues of high art versus low art, you couldn't possibly put in some of these scenes.

Do you see yourself following earlier dancers in creating these comic circus scenes?

Tandy Beal in rehearsal. Photo by Terry Lorant.

One of my mentors, Murray Louis, had a wonderful comic persona. But generally in the dance world, I've always felt like an outsider. I would love to feel that I was part of a tradition of eccentric dancers! As I think about it, there is an eclectic group of people with one foot in dance and one in "comic circus." Lotte Goslar mined a rich vein of imagination that was at the cusp of clowning and dance. Katie Litz was another wonderfully zany dancer. Mitchell Rose was very funny; I think he left the dance world because there was very little support for that kind of performance. I think if he had been in the circus, he'd still be performing; he was really funny in his take on things. I'd love to set up a series for eccentric dances and see them all under the same umbrella. It would call people out of the woodwork. Starting something like that might, in fact, be a way to find and encourage clowns.

Kimi Okada and some of the other Pickles have drawn on the tradition of eccentric dance in their circus work, but I'm not sure it has received much critical recognition as a continuation of earlier vaudeville dance forms. In any case, the dances are not "normal" circus practice in our culture, either. Audiences expect an older, more traditional circus, with animals and death-defying acts, for the most part. As circuses go, the Pickles are "an outsider" too.

I think you're right. Pickles have been a bit of an outsider throughout the years. I can only address what I know during my time here—although clearly the no-animal policy that Pickles adhered to vigorously since the beginning is now one that many circuses are following. And we still do. Another tradition that was started early was first-rate clowning with Larry, Geoff, and Bill. Now these are definitely big shoes to fill, but Jeff and Diane have done it well. It has been a great treat to work together again this year.

We started touring in theatres about ten years ago—also somewhat of a departure for circus. Since I come from a theatre/dance background, that was an easy direction for me to maintain. I love the coordination of all the elements to make a show, adding to the acts music, lights, costumes, color, and choreography. And yet my intention is to make our shows feel warm and intimate, with a sense of wonder and delight. Something we could all use more of . . .

The Pickle budget may not be as large as that of other circuses, but the Pickles have continually offered artists opportunities not available elsewhere to be involved creatively in the production process.

I think the Cirque [du Soleil] has done an astonishing job "theatricalizing" circus. But maybe one of the historical differences is that the Pickles are human-sized, both in the show and in the making of it.

The public has an increasing appetite that demands higher and higher skill levels and huge production values—it's the Andrew Lloyd Weber syndrome! These are forces that are shaping an audience's expectations. And, of course, we have to contend with it too.

The thing about the Pickles is the feeling that this can be an artistic home. Rather than come in, do your act, and leave, it is a place where, through yeasty collaborations, people can develop their acts and themselves even more. It is sometimes hard to tell where one person's idea starts and the next one's begins. There can be a great joy in the synergy of working like this.

It's not just a question of scale but also one of freedom for the artist; I think there's a more centralized artistic control and less collaboration among artists in Cirque.

I think that one of my jobs, as well as one of my gifts, is that I can put banks to somebody's river so that they're not just flooding the plain with abundant ideas. I can usually hear what they're saying, keep us on course, and keep finding structure. It's always labor-intensive to make something; but I love it when people are bringing in their *esprit* and investing themselves in the process.

Dancers are quick to learn things, quicker on the surface than circus people. In circus, the performer often starts out with an impossible idea (like standing on her head on her partner's head while they are balancing on a rolla bolla). I remain in awe of people who attempt to do something that seems impossible, and [in fact] they can't do [the particular skill] for a year or longer. But they still try it every day, over and over. Finally, when they get it, it's this miracle, and it comes about through astonishingly hard work. And then all of the artists—the composer, designers, director—work to enhance that trick, that metaphor, even more.

In the role of director, though, you have to have a practical sensibility, like it or not. The practical grounding is going to allow the dreams to take shape. That's one reason I said we should do a Pickle show for two years. From the performer's point of view, after the show has been on the road for a year, it's seasoned, you know where the beats are, you've gotten rid of the dead wood, you've refined things with an audience. In the second year of *Tossing and Turning* and *Jump Cuts!*, quite a few acts changed; we were able to adjust them, and the whole show got tighter.

I wish we could be in a situation where we could contract the performers for two or three years. But right now we can't.

At least you've been able to bring some of the same artists back to the Pickles from season to season, however seasonal the work.

Now some of them have been picked up by Cirque du Soleil. They call themselves "The San Francisco Seven." And that's just for one Cirque show. However, we can't afford to keep training people just so they come to the level that Cirque will want.

This year, in addition to some of our own local artists, I am going to bring in very seasoned performers. With these Russian and Chinese artists, there are no training issues involved. We'll have the best acrobatic performers we've ever had, as well as clowns.

The New Pickle Circus has become more international in its composition in recent years. As you mentioned in an earlier conversation, in the circus, artists from different countries work together with cooperation that politicians take much longer to achieve.

When I worked for the Moscow Circus in Japan, there were many problems. I would get in despair and wonder if I would ever get the show up. Then I'd look at the fact that these three countries were at war not fifty years ago, and here we are trying to make something beautiful for people's families to enjoy. We *had* to make it work, because if we couldn't make it work, then you can't possibly talk about peace as a reality. That sustained me as a metaphor, as an image, to get up with every morning and go into the fracas!

I'm very pleased that in our small circus—a total of twenty people including crew and band—again this year we'll have four different languages and bring in different ways of looking at the world. I love that aspect of it.

It's the future of our planet in microcosm, working it out together as an organization that has to function together, with people from different cultures depending on each other.

There's still a place for clowns in this scheme?

Thank God for it. When I was much younger, I thought the important part of life was serious: a serious book, a serious relationship, a serious piece of art. As I've gotten older, I've realized it's laughter that gets you through. Laughter is the divine gift. Of all the gifts, the best is if you can laugh at life yourself. You are even better if you can help other people laugh. I'm not sure there's a greater gift than that.

I heard the Dalai Lama say something that I love. Someone asked him, "Could you describe enlightenment?" The Dalai Lama took a beat and said, "Well, the best way I can describe enlightenment is spontaneous laughter."

That could lead to much more widespread appreciation of clowns.

Yes, it could. When you're part of an audience that's laughing together, it's an amazing event. As I'm telling you about this, I realize this is so much the reason I work in the circus office until eleven at night and get up at six and start it again. It's a great gift, if you can allow people a moment of relief from the dailiness of their lives with a moment of laughter or wonder. I love it when I can find a poetic moment, a moment of beauty as well as a moment of humor, that can just take your breath away.

Appendix A

Appendix B

Index

Appendix A

Pickle Circus Clowns, 1975–2000

Year	Clowns	Circus Director[a]
1975	Pisoni, Irwin, Okada, Hoyle	Pisoni
1976	Pisoni, Irwin, Okada, Mankin, Forrest, Hoyle	
1977	Pisoni, Irwin, Hoyle	
1978	Pisoni, Irwin, Hoyle	
1979	Pisoni, Hoyle, Snow	
1980	Pisoni, Hoyle	
1981	Pisoni, Hoyle	
1981	Pisoni, Irwin, Hoyle (winter season/*Three High*)	Richard Seyd
1982	Pisoni, Lorenzo Pisoni, Wendy Parkman, Gypsy Snider, Derique McGee, Marc Jondall	Pisoni
1983	Pisoni, Lorenzo Pisoni, Judy Finelli, Gypsy Snider, Marc Jondall, Derique McGee, Jim Murdock	
1984	Pisoni, Lorenzo Pisoni, Hoyle (in December), Marc Jondall, Derique McGee, Robin Hood, Peggy Snider, Gypsy Snider, Jean Paul Valjean	
1985	Jack Golden, Sharon Ostreicher	
1986	Pisoni, Lorenzo Pisoni	
1987	Pisoni, Lorenzo Pisoni, Hoyle (in December)	Judy Finelli
1988	Mankin, Forrest	
1989	Mankin, Wasnak	
1990	Mankin, Wasnak	
1991	Wasnak, Raz	Pisoni
1992	Wasnak, Raz	Beal
1993	Wasnak, Raz	
1994	Wasnak, Raz	
1995	Wasnak, Raz	
1996	Raz, Keith Terry	
1997	Joseph Kreinke, Stephanie Thompson	
1998	Wasnak, Raz, Amos Glick	
1999	Wasnak, San Francisco School of Circus Arts students	Lu Yi/Beal
2000	Raz, Wasnak, Rob Rodgers	Beal/Lu Yi

[a]Only changes are noted after 1975.

Appendix B
A Catalog of Pickle Clown Acts

Musical Clown Acts

The Three Musicians. Hoyle, Irwin, and Pisoni prepare to play a concert; briefly play.
Tubas and Violins. Hoyle, Pisoni, and Snow sit on each other and play "Lady of Spain."
Tuba Trunks. Hoyle emerges from trunk, tubas emerge, Hoyle and Pisoni play them.
Saxophones. Mankin and Wasnak differ on choice of instruments, then play sax duet
    and are joined by Lorenzo Pisoni in gorilla suit; all dance.
La La Luna Sea. Mankin steals Wasnak's saxophone; long search for it follows.

Clowns with Gorillas

Tap-Dancing Gorilla. Okada in suit turns tables on trainer (Irwin); forces him to dance.
Gorillas. Nine to twelve performers in suits get Pisoni to join them in dance. (Also see
    Saxophones above.)

Clowns in Eccentric Dances

Willy's Hat Dive. Irwin does short welcome dance and dives into top hat; it stays on
    his head.
Horned Hat Dance. Hoyle and Pisoni wear tall white fur hats with horns; dance.
Reunion Dance. Hoyle, Pisoni, Irwin try to dance in unison; fall into orchestra pit.
Boing Boing Boogie Woogie Bounce. Hoyle boogies and is a human bouncing ball.
Let's Face the Music and . . . Wasnak and Raz dance, he in strapless gown, she in tux.
Midnight Munchies. Raz as insomniac watches tomato sandwich dance past him.

Clowns in Trunks

Dueling Trunks. Hoyle and Irwin walk downstairs in their separate trunks.
Multiple Sniffs. Four to seven clowns dressed like Sniff keep coming out of trunks.
Trunks. Hoyle saws Irwin's cane, pushes him into trunk, considers sawing off Irwin's
    leg.
Tuba Trunks. (see above under Musical Clown Acts)
Gepetto. Lorenzo Pisoni and dummy emerge from trunk; both look like Lorenzo Pickle.
Lorenzo Finds an Old Friend. "Heavy" trunk holds light balloons offered to spectator.

Clowns in Cafés, Restaurants

Spaghetti. Served with difficulty by waiter (Irwin) and chef (Pisoni, later Hoyle).
Ralph and Queenie's Kitchen. Forrest tries to follow Mankin's recipe and cook chicken.
Café des Artistes. Turn-of-the-century French café where everyone is a circus artist.

Parodies of Other Circus Acts

Sniff the Magnificent. Hoyle is bogus weight lifter, Pisoni his assistant.

The Human Cannon. Hoyle is shot out of cannon inside Palace of Fine Arts.

Magician. Golden tries to make his assistant, Ostreicher, vanish inside a box and has difficulty.

Magician's Assistant. Mankin spoils magic tricks attempted by Steve LaBounty.

Other Animals (Besides Gorillas) Impersonated

Sandsniff. Hoyle resembles a rare bird sought by ornithologist Snow.

The Big Buzz. Wasnak is mosquito; Raz is disturbed by it.

Lummox. Hoyle meets big, doglike creature.

Goldilocks. Wasnak portrays young girl and three bears who eat her; speaks in gibberish.

Acts That Defy Other Categories

Ace Moving Men. Hoyle, Irwin, Pisoni try not to destroy furniture they move for widow (Cecil MacKinnon) who keeps husband's ashes in a vase.

The Wedding Photo. Irwin is photographer; Hoyle, the bride; Pisoni, the groom.

The Human Pillow. Raz tries to sleep; Wasnak is uncooperative pillow.

Electra, the Demon Baby from Hell. Wasnak escapes baby carriage; Mankin pursues.

Teetertots. Wasnak as infant joins other acrobats; Raz has to catch her.

Planks. Forrest and Mankin hold wooden boards; she narrowly misses him in turning.

Auntie Elvie. Wasnak as elderly woman in unstable rocking chair.

Index

Winter, Doug, 68
Woodruff, Robert, 140, 145

Yengebarov, Leonid, 25–26

Zanni, 8
Zappa, Frank, 156
Zazlov, Arnie, 105

Joel Schechter is a professor of theatre arts at San Francisco State University. His previous books include *Durov's Pig: Clowns, Politics and Theatre; Satiric Impersonations: From Aristophanes to the Guerrilla Girls;* and *The Congress of Clowns and Other Russian Circus Acts.* He has served as the editor of the journal *Theater,* as West Coast correspondent for the circus quarterly *Spectacle,* and as a faculty member at the Yale School of Drama, the State University of New York at Stony Brook, and New York University's Department of Performance Studies.